BENEATH THE RESTLESS WAVE

Memoirs of a Cold War Submariner

TONY BEASLEY
with EDWARD COUZENS-LAKE

CASEMATE

Oxford & Philadelphia

Published in Great Britain and the United States of America in 2020 by
CASEMATE PUBLISHERS
The Old Music Hall, 106–108 Cowley Road, Oxford OX4 1JE, UK
and
1950 Lawrence Road, Havertown, PA 19083, US

Hardcover Edition: ISBN 978-1-61200-840-0
Digital Edition: ISBN 978-1-61200-841-7

A CIP record for this book is available from the British Library

Printed and bound in the United Kingdom by TJ International

Typeset in India for Casemate Publishing Services. www.casematepublishingservices.com

For a complete list of Casemate titles, please contact:

CASEMATE PUBLISHERS (UK)
Telephone (01865) 241249
Email: casemate-uk@casematepublishers.co.uk
www.casematepublishers.co.uk

CASEMATE PUBLISHERS (US)
Telephone (610) 853-9131
Fax (610) 853-9146
Email: casemate@casematepublishers.com
www.casematepublishers.com

The views and opinions expressed are those of the author alone and should not be taken to represent those of Her Majesty's Government, MOD, HM Armed Forces or any government agency.

Contents

To Katie

Introduction

Tony Beasley is a remarkable man.

He's like a character from one of the classic old British or US comic books come to life: maybe one of Superman's best buddies, the straight-talking Navy man who always told Superman the truth, even if it wasn't what he wanted to hear. I'm not sure that Tony would appreciate the comparison but at least I know that if he doesn't, he'll soon let me know. The so-called golden era of children's comics such as those, complete with their tough, lantern-jawed heroes like Union Jack Jackson, The Flash and Captain America, were fiction of course. Yet their heroes served as role models for a generation, revered because they were loyal, tough and unwavering in their duty. Each one a man's man, as the saying goes.

Tony didn't come out of the pages of a comic. But he is, for me, that kind of man who, when I was growing up, I would have wanted to be: someone to look up to, to respect and admire for what he did in life and the way he went about it. He really is the young boy who ran away from home to go to sea, a life in service that began when he walked up the gangplank to join his first ship as a boy telegraphist in 1950.

It was a time when both Great Britain's Royal Navy and the nation itself were recovering and rebuilding, a mere five years after a hard-won peace in Japan had finally brought to an end the horrors and devastation of the Second World War. Little did Tony, or any of his contemporaries, know that they would soon be sailing into the teeth of another war, one that saw no fighting but which was still, nevertheless, as potentially deadly as those which had preceded it.

I am, of course, talking about the Cold War. Tony played his part in that clandestine duel between East and West in a way that he would never have expected or asked to do, an account of which he shares with the reader in the pages that follow.

The recollections and memories of his life, as both a boy and a man, are told with brutal honesty, as are his observations relating to the people, places and situations he has found himself in over the course of his life. Tony doesn't hold back: he tells things as he sees them, something he has never been afraid of doing, even if it gives someone a bloody nose in the process, his own included.

It's a remarkable story, one I feel immensely privileged to have shared with him.

I hope it is one that you enjoy reading as much as I have enjoyed writing it.

Edward Couzens-Lake

Prologue

I'm writing my story because it needs to be told.

It's honest and doesn't pull any punches. It won't be pretty in places whilst, in others, it may be decidedly uncomfortable. It is not, by any stretch of the imagination, meant to be politically correct and is riddled, throughout, with Royal Navy slang, joviality and innuendo. If the language and phrases used are sometimes harsh or even shocking to the reader, then I offer no apology.

Why am I writing it? Because I want to portray the struggle I encountered against the mighty weight of the establishment, one I fought despite all the odds being very heavily stacked against me. I have, throughout, endeavoured to stick with facts rather than hyperbole, facts that are backed, where appropriate, by documentary evidence.

The facts are that I was injured in an accident on a British submarine during a covert mission. As the years went on the injury continued to cause me severe pain, but my records did not detail the cause of the injury because my MoD records deliberately omitted the fact that I ever served in submarines. The official account of the injury, in other words, is designed to fit in with MoD requirements and to be recorded with their convenience in mind, rather than that of the affected party. The fight to get my injuries recognised and a suitable award took many years. Moreover, the treatment I received from Norcross NX, the branch of the MoD that processes injuries incurred whilst serving with the military, showed me that it has a very different attitude to officers and other ranks. I fought for a long time at significant personal cost to get justice.

Those of us who live a long life can look back and pick out the episodes that were pivotal in directing the course of our life story. From the wartime experiences of my boyhood to my escapades as a young seaman, then the activities I undertook – voluntarily or not – in service to the Royal Navy and my country as an adult, every chapter in this book takes the reader a step closer to understanding where I am today, and why I chose to fight against official indifference to my circumstances.

It is because of these circumstances that I want my story written, read and shared. I am, with it, now prepared to approach the media or anyone else interested in learning more about it – and, crucially, on my terms, no one else's. The time is right. I am over eighty years old and living on borrowed time. Yet this incredible story, written over a long period of the time I have already had, will not die with me, that I promise you.

You can read on and come to your own conclusions now.

Tony Beasley

CHAPTER I

Mum, What's War?

'We must all have seen and heard it at the same time: a German fighter plane with black smoke belching from one of its engines plummeting down to the ground about three or four miles away from where we were and close to, as it turned out, the main Brighton to London railway line.'

On Sunday September 3rd 1939 the Prime Minister, Neville Chamberlain, made an announcement that would change the way of life for countless millions of people all over the world.

I am speaking to you from the cabinet room at 10 Downing Street. This morning the British ambassador in Berlin handed the German government a final note stating that unless we heard from them by 11 o'clock that they were prepared at once to withdraw their troops from Poland, a state of war would exist between us. I have to tell you now that no such undertaking has been received, and that consequently this country is at war with Germany.

Neville Chamberlain must have believed that he had done everything in his power to prevent the country being hurled into a potentially catastrophic global conflict, one that had erupted around him a little over two decades after another had drawn to its own bloody conclusion. The Great War had precipitated the solemnity of the Cenotaph; poppies; the well-worn phrase 'the war to end all wars' and a common understanding amongst all of humanity that such a war could and should never happen again. For years Chamberlain had done what he must have thought was his best to halt a repeat war with Germany. This included a foreign policy that preached appeasement and which, ultimately, saw him concede the

German-speaking Sudetenland region of Czechoslovakia to Germany in 1938. That, Chamberlain must have thought, will be that. Hitler and his Nazi Germany will be content with their new empire and will have neither the heart nor the desire to fight another war. Yet, fuelling the resentment towards the rest of Europe that had been ignited by the Treaty of Versailles in 1919, Hitler's annexation of the Sudetenland was just the start and, when his forces invaded Britain's ally Poland, Chamberlain could no longer offer appeasement, talks and negotiation.

It was time for war.

I was a six-year-old lad at the time. I heard the news but have to admit, it didn't really strike much of a chord to me. And why would it? Many things catch the mind and imagination of six-year-old scallywag boys, but world politics is not one of them. Thus, as I returned home from Sunday School that fine and sunny morning, I remember managing to scrape up just enough interest in what everyone was talking about to offer my Mum a question, shouted aloud as I passed the open kitchen window.

'Mum, what's war?'

Eighty years have come and gone since I asked her that innocent question. The Second World War feels long, long ago. But it is a time I will never forget. Neither, of course, will the village we lived in, tightly nestled in the heart of the English countryside, as remote as it could be from the horrors and grim reality of the real world. Except even that had changed as, one by one, the young men who had been born, raised and started their working lives there steadily became more and more conspicuous by their absence. And this war was different to any that had been fought before. It wasn't reserved exclusively for the battlefields, nor were the combatants and casualties exclusively those who wore a uniform and bore arms. People witnessed this war, felt it and suffered from its effects on their doorsteps as the Luftwaffe brought a campaign of sustained bombing attacks to many of Britain's towns and cities. London, of course, became a very obvious and high-profile target for repeated raids, with the first of those that went onto be known as the Blitz occurring on the night of September 7th 1940.

If I hadn't known what war was when it was declared by Chamberlain on that sunny Sunday morning, then I and tens of thousands of innocents most certainly did after that dreadful day.

You didn't need to live in London to know and see what was happening there. We lived in Horsted Keynes, a small Sussex village that lies around five miles north-east of the larger town of Haywards Heath and about 40 miles south of London. Did that make the war out of sight and out of mind for me and everyone who was living there? No. When there was enough power in the radio batteries we heard, via the BBC, of the dreadful loss of life and damage the Luftwaffe raids were causing, especially to the dockside areas where so many people lived and worked. The red glow of the raging fires in London's East End was clearly visible to us, night after night, as we looked northwards towards the capital over the spire of St Giles church from the roadway outside the blacksmith's shop on the village green. So we knew how terribly London suffered.

That church, I have to admit, proved to be a bit of an attraction to me and my friends during those early years. If you went inside it, you couldn't help but notice the narrow iron ladder that hung ever so invitingly down, close to the vicar's pulpit. Now, with a bit of ingenuity (and I was never short of that), I found that you could jump or lean across the pulpit, catch the bottom rung of this ladder and pull yourself up it from there. The climb then took you upwards to two further ladders that led to the hidden realm of the bell tower where, amongst the bells, silent now and only to be rung in the event of invasion, there were other, living occupants, including the ubiquitous pigeons, an occasional owl and assorted creepy crawlies of all kinds. That meant, of course, that there was mess up there. And I mean mess. Every nook and cranny of that tower's interior was covered in a rich mix of dead birds, egg shells, excrement, cobwebs and feathers. Yet, in all its gloriously filthy and odorous abundance, the mess didn't really bother us that much. Our reason for climbing up into the tower and the interior of the steeple was to find a gap from where we could get a better view of those raging fires that were destroying our proud capital. It was, for us youngsters, something exciting – and we wanted the best view the village could offer us.

On this occasion, however, that childhood ingenuity did not pay off as there were no gaps in the steeple that we could look through. So, slightly disappointed, we decided to call it a day and started to climb back down the ladders with one of the girls in our little exploration party leading the way. And, for a while, everything seemed to be going smoothly. That is, until we tried to negotiate our way back out of the bottom hatchway where the second of the three ladders would become reachable. I still don't know the reason why there was a sudden outbreak of panic amongst those of us who were forming the vanguard but that barely mattered. What *did* matter was the result of that panic: someone at the front of the group reaching out and inadvertently grabbing one of the bell ropes.

The noise that suddenly came from that long-silent bell made us all panic even more, and this time for a very understandable reason. The four of us slid down the bell ropes to the floor amidst the increasing cacophony, loud enough now to wake the dead or, more to the point, the village. By the time we reached the floor again, all of the bells were ringing which could only mean one thing. The good people of Horsted Keynes would now be thinking that the country was being invaded.

We scrambled, in an almost blind panic, out of the church and into the graveyard, making a beeline for a place that we'd often used as a sanctuary when we'd ended up being chased for scrumping apples from a nearby orchard. This was a partially ruined mausoleum that stood, largely forgotten, in the church grounds. We thought we'd be able to hide out there in safety for a while before innocently making our respective ways home and wondering what all the fuss had been about.

As we all crouched, still and silent, in the comforting darkness of the mausoleum, I was able, by looking through one of the numerous cracks in the walls, to see the lychgate[1] at the entrance of the church grounds. This was normally part of a quiet and tranquil village scene, one that radiated peace and quiet. But we'd changed all that and the activity that was now beginning to intensify around that gate was building up at such

---

1 A roofed gateway to a churchyard, formerly used at burials for sheltering a coffin until the clergyman's arrival.

a rate of knots that we were all now in danger of wetting ourselves in spectacular and copious unison.

True to form, the first person to arrive on the scene was PC Franks astride his trusty two-wheeled steed. Bad enough as far as we were concerned. But he didn't come alone for, shortly after he arrived, an army lorry, bursting to capacity with eager soldiers, turned up, with some of them seemingly so eager to apprehend the enemy they fell over one another as they got off their noisy transport. This little bit of slapstick might, under normal circumstances, have given us all a good laugh but seeing them there with their rifles at the ready served only to frighten us even more. Yet as we remained frozen to the spot and silent in that tumbledown mausoleum, our levels of fear escalated even higher when we noticed that all of the noise we'd made and resultant activity had, inevitably, led to the usual array of village do-gooders and gossips arriving on the scene. They were all chattering away, nineteen to the dozen, offering up, no doubt, their own explanations as to what or who was behind all the cacophony. It was the sort of unruly mob that always turned up for a public lynching or, worse still, an execution. They, along with the soldiers and PC Franks, would all be aware that the ringing of church bells during wartime could mean only one thing: enemy parachutists. Their blood was up and, sooner or later, we'd have to face the consequences.

Petrified doesn't even begin to describe how I was feeling at that point. Yes, we were young. But not so young that we didn't realise the seriousness of what we had done and the possible implications for all of us when we were eventually caught and dragged out to face PC Franks, the armed soldiers and, worst of all, the angry villagers. We remained in our hiding place, the combination of the gathering chill in the air and our fear meaning that we were all shaking so much, I feared that someone would hear us and reveal our hiding place. But no: luck, or rather PC Franks, was on our side for, after what seemed an eternity, our knowing and experienced village bobby was able to convince the soldiers that, as far as he was concerned, the whole thing was down to some kids 'mucking about' and that everyone should calm down and go about their business, the soldiers included. After a few more muttered conversations, they agreed with him, got back onto their lorries and disappeared back to their barracks, disappointed, perhaps, that they were not, after all, going into battle against the enemy on the streets of Horsted Keynes. More importantly, at least as far as our little quartet were concerned, it meant that we probably weren't going to end up being shot after all.

Dark and dangerous as those times were for everyone, a war, like it or not, provides an endless source of fascination and even amusement for children, too young to really understand all its implications yet at the same time old enough to make the very most of the opportunities that it presents from time to time. And this was, for me and my friends, never more evident than in those long summer days in 1940 which saw the Battle of Britain fought out on a daily basis in the skies above southern England. Had Hitler's German forces triumphed in their attempts to nullify British air superiority at this time then the war would have taken a very different course. Defeat for the RAF would almost certainly have been a prelude to that much feared invasion of this country along its eastern and southern coasts, with the implications of that rather too terrible, even today, to contemplate. The villagers would have heard those church bells rung for a very real and terrifying reason then. Fortunately, the RAF, 'the few', prevailed and, although the war dragged on for five more years, the possibility of this country being invaded was, for at least the short term, nullified. Not that, as I have already mentioned, we children were aware of that or living in the same kind of fear that our parents and grandparents were.

For us, the blue skies above Sussex were a bright and brilliant canvas where we would watch our fastest fighter aircraft, the Spitfires and Hurricanes, engaged in combat with the German fighter escorts. These were usually Messerschmitt 109s, detailed to accompany the large and majestic bomber aircraft that had been sent over the English Channel from occupied France with orders to bomb our naval dockyards in Portsmouth and Plymouth as well as numerous RAF airfields based in Kent, Hampshire and Sussex. Many people are, of course, familiar with the terrible damage and accordant loss of life that occurred in London as a result of the Blitz, but many other cities were also very badly affected. Portsmouth was hit by 67 separate air raids between July 1940 and May

1944, attacks that destroyed 6,625 houses as well as causing severe damage to a further 6,549.

Portsmouth was a major target of the Luftwaffe for several reasons. It was home to countless military and industrial installations as well as being home to the Royal Navy. In that four-year period, 930 people were killed and 1,216 needed hospital treatment whilst a further 1,621 suffered less severe injuries. Attacks such as these were made because the Nazi leaders believed that a prolonged campaign of bombing against British cities would, ultimately, lead to the populace putting more and more pressure on the government to find a peaceful resolution to the conflict. The British Government, however, saw these raids as an inevitable price to pay for war and, rather than look to sue for peace with Hitler, sought, instead, to find ways of lessening the damage to our major cities that these raids caused. As far as Portsmouth was concerned, and, presumably much to the horror of the residents of nearby Hayling Island, less populated areas, such as Hayling, were deliberately used as decoys for the German bombers. This meant the construction of temporary buildings all over the island which then had their lights left on so that they were easily visible to raiding aircraft. In other less strategic (i.e. more remote) areas, fires were lit to mimic the effect of incendiary devices in order to 'lure' the bombers to these false targets. Hayling Island therefore suffered greatly during this phase of the war but it did mean that there was, ultimately, less damage and loss of life in the more densely populated areas of Portsmouth.

The Luftwaffe's terrifyingly clinical flying machines always seemed to be flying in picture-perfect formation with their large back cross insignias proudly placed on their fuselage. To us, those aircraft gave off the distinct impression that they genuinely thought they owned the sky, that it was theirs to dominate and do whatever they liked in – wherever they were. If it hadn't been for those brave and selfless pilots from the RAF and other countries around the world during the Battle of Britain, of course, they would have succeeded and the sky really would have belonged to the Luftwaffe and Nazi Germany. Yet, as children, such thoughts were far from our minds, and we contented ourselves with watching them fly overhead on their murderous quests to cause havoc on our still free, green and pleasant land, sometimes having bets amongst ourselves as to how many aircraft were in each group as they slowly but resolutely droned overhead. Quite often, in amongst all of the myriad vapour trails that crisscrossed the blue skies, we'd notice a trail of black smoke slowly descending earthwards, an image that requires no further description. Sometimes we'd notice the glint of sunshine on a parachute as an airman who'd managed to get out of his burning aircraft made his escape, one that must have been a terrifying journey back to terra firma. Needless to say, those flyers were not always enemy ones.

One afternoon a gang of us were playing around the yew trees that separated the school playground from the churchyard. We'd noticed something going on in the north side of the churchyard and, when we were able to take a closer look, came across a sight the memory of which causes me upset to this day.[2] Looking more closely, we witnessed two dead German airmen being hastily buried and with little to no respect being given to them in the process.

I didn't, of course, think so at the time yet today, that incident and the awful images that I saw that afternoon flood back into my mind whenever I happen to casually look upwards and notice the numerous contrails made by the commercial airliners that crisscross the sky, coming and going from the modern-day Gatwick Airport which is just under 60 miles from where I live today.

It's a mental and emotional picture, a flashback that still makes me shake with emotion and rage. How, I ask myself, could people act so insensibly? Yes, it was a time of war. Yes, we hated the Germans for the destruction and carnage that they were carrying out throughout Europe – but that did not excuse, did not get away from the fact that

---

2 The incident that the author witnessed came about after a Messerschmitt Bf109E-4 was shot down in combat with Hurricanes over East Grinstead on September 30th 1940. It crashed into a pond on Cinderhill Farm in Horsted Keynes at 9:45am with both crewmen discovered dead in the wreckage. The pilot's name was Hans Bertram of 2 *Staffel* (Squadron) with his wingman named as Alfred Sander, also of 2 *Staffel*. The two men were interred in plot 1, grave 1 in a reserved area of St Giles Church in Horsted Keynes before later being re-interred in Block 1, Grave 17 of the *Soldatenfriedhof* (Military Cemetery) at Cannock Chase in Staffordshire.

these men were somebody's sons, husbands or fathers, doing what they had been ordered to do by their egotistical leaders. They had no choice; they had to carry out those orders for fear of the most harsh of reprisals if they refused, either against them or members of their families. You'd think, of course, that things have changed since then and that we are all a lot more civilised about such things today but, regretfully, that same scenario carries on even now and on our own doorsteps. How I would love to be able to read the history books that will be written about these times in, say, fifty years' time.

Another incident I remember happened late one summer's afternoon as we were returning home after helping with the picking of raspberries that were destined to be turned into jam at St Martin's jam factory. We must all have seen and heard it at the same time: a German fighter plane with black smoke belching from one of its engines plummeting down to the ground about three or four miles away from where we were and close to, as it turned out, the main Brighton to London railway line. Several of us immediately raced off to the crash site on our bikes, where we found still-smoking pieces of the wrecked aircraft spread over a relatively small area.

As was the curious and devil-may-care attitude of small boys at the time, we all wanted a souvenir and we didn't hesitate to plunder the spoils, each of us grabbing a piece of the smashed plastic windshield and making off like lighting with our plunder tied to our bikes. We were just in time as well, for, just as we left, a few more interested parties arrived on the scene, all of them carrying rifles and looking like they were ready for anything. But we didn't immediately rush back; there was a row of walnut trees growing near the scene of the crash so we briefly stopped to fill our pockets with nuts before proceeding. I had hoped that I would find a parachute for Mum so that she could make some clothes out of the material as she had done on another occasion, but, sadly, no such luck this time. Still, we knew that someone would be able to make use of what we had found so we made our way to the Italian POW camp at Pax Hill, which was about three miles from the village. The POWs welcomed any materials that they could use in order to make rings, brooches and other imitation cosmetic jewellery. There was a German POW camp on the opposite side of the road to where the Italians were but that was strictly out of bounds to everyone, and this was one instruction that we were not going to disregard.

And that was that. Or so we thought at the time. For, a few days later, PC Franks visited the school and spoke to us all at assembly, asking if anyone had seen or visited the site of the crashed Luftwaffe aircraft near the railway line. It turned out that someone had found the altimeter[3] at the crash site and made off with it. This was a vital piece of equipment and had to be found. So who had it? But not a word. No one stirred and silence reigned. But PC Franks was not to be denied. From his lofty vantage point on our school stage, our hawk-eyed policeman noticed that one of the girls in the front row had a large stain on her hands.

He then whispered something to Mrs Morse, our dreaded headmistress, notifying her of what he had seen and that it suggested that something was amiss. The girl was promptly called up onto the stage to show her hands to Mrs Morse and to explain how that treacherous stain, the unmistakable result of a walnut feast, had come to be there. Whilst this was going on, PC Franks stalked the lines between the desks, noting, as he did, some other children were nervously fidgeting in their places and, in doing so, trying their utmost to hide their hands. The game was up and he had an answer to his question. But, as for what happened to that missing altimeter, it remained a mystery.

***

It was around about the summer of 1943 when the appearance and geography of the countryside around our peaceful little village changed. And this was due to an invasion. It wasn't, of course, one spearheaded by German parachutists, so there was no need for the church bells to be rung. No, the invading army was made up of Canadian soldiers who were appearing in increasingly high numbers and settling down in an

---

3 An altimeter is an instrument used to measure the altitude of an object above a fixed level.

assortment of camps all around us, some of them in places that we'd never seen or heard about, let alone thought suitable for a camp.

The Canadians were a welcome sight. Not only did their large and friendly presence symbolise the strength of the Allied cause in terms of friendly nations who were only too willing to send their own troops and equipment to help fight and win the war, but also because it meant that we were preparing for an invasion of our own. It was all top secret of course — but why else would they be there? Things had been very different three years earlier when the whole nation had been living in dread of a Nazi invasion. No one was speculating on whether it might take place or not; we were certain it was going to happen. That was the very reason why the nation's church bells, including our own, had been silenced and would only be pealed if enemy invasion was imminent or under way. France had capitulated in 1940, less than a year into the conflict and, with most of western Europe under Nazi control, Britain had seemed the next logical step for Hitler's expansionist plans.

Hitler had already been able to celebrate one victory over Britain. In retreat and trapped on the beaches at Dunkirk, British forces, with high losses in both terms of personnel and equipment, had fled back across the English Channel, beaten and in some disarray. At this point in time, Hitler probably thought that there would be no need to invade Britain at all and that Winston Churchill would, rather than surrendering entirely, sue for a peace, albeit on terms that suited Nazi Germany more than it did Britain. It would mean that Britain remained an independent nation, albeit one that was no more than a vassal island to a massive continental Empire. But one that was still, to all intents and purposes, 'free' from tyranny and subjugation.

Much to Hitler's surprise however, the British government and people showed zero appetite for such a deal. Which left him with two options: to either blockade Britain as much as possible and, over time, psychologically wear down the nation into, finally, accepting a deal, or to invade and conquer.

Hence everyone's feelings of reassurance in reaction to the friendly 'invasion' from our Canadian allies. And what a contribution they ended up making. It's rather too easy to see that terrible conflict as being fought solely between the Axis powers of Nazi Germany, Italy and Japan against those from Europe and the USA but, in truth, if you count up the Allied powers who were engaged in the fighting, together with the nations who supported them, the total involved comes to nearly forty countries. Hence it was, rightly, called a *world* war. The Canadian Armed Forces played a huge and very active role in the fighting, especially in Italy, north-western Europe and the North Atlantic, with a total of over one million Canadians serving in the Canadian Army, Royal Canadian Navy and the Royal Canadian Air Force. They lost approximately 42,000 serving personnel during the conflict with another 55,000 wounded. The nation of Canada even, at one point, 'saw' direct action within its own borders at the Battle of the St Lawrence, an ongoing marine and anti-submarine action that took place throughout the lower St Lawrence River as well as the entire Gulf of St Lawrence.

I wonder how many of those brave young boys I saw training in the relative peace and quiet of the Sussex countryside ended up dying for their mother nation and never seeing home again.

The area of Horsted Keynes, famous for the nearby scenic Bluebell Railway line, was turning out to be a much larger playground than most of us had initially thought and, as a result, our own perceptions of the world around us were beginning, irrevocably, to change as the Canadian soldiers began to settle down and make themselves known in that part of that world. The area that they had chosen was around three lakes on an area known as the Broadhurst estate which belonged to a man called Johnny Clark. This land was situated a few hundred yards west of the church so it was very much part of the village; indeed, the largest of the three lakes on that piece of land was known as the Swimming Lake and would be the first that you would come across if you were exploring the area. Next, and a little bit lower down, was a smaller and shallower lake, about the size of a small and muddy pond. It fed excess water to the third and final lake, which was known as the Mill Lake. This was about the same size as the Swimming Lake but was a lot more shallow and full of weeds. It was a popular and attractive spot which was set off very nicely by the presence of a watermill at its southern border.

The lakes were surrounded by mature oak trees, all many hundreds of years old, straddling the green mossy banks with some growing right at the water's edge. Those trees and the surrounding vegetation were a wonderful haven for moorhen, coot, ducks and a myriad of other species, the only real threat to their way of life coming from the ever wily Reynard the fox who, you could be sure, would be lurking with intent behind some shrub or other with hunger in his heart. Several pairs of swans could be seen every spring proudly showing off their cygnets, resplendent in their brownish plumage, camouflaged among in the reeds that grew in abundance around the Mill Lake. Fishing was banned because of the very real risk to the health of the swans and other birds that could all too easily get entangled in the catgut and hooks that might be left behind by a careless angler. We were able to catch eels by a waterfall that was opposite the watermill, but we had to do this by hand, a risky undertaking since eels bite – and it hurts!

On the west side of the lake was an apple and plum orchard as well as two greengage trees, discreetly hidden in a secret corner. It was all very much the essence of that 'green and pleasant land', the England that our local men were fighting for. It was now also a place that those Canadian soldiers were fighting for, whose presence in our village and down by the lakes was set to change things so much. Where there had been peace and tranquility, empty streets and birdsong, were now motor vehicles, many with tank tracks, some of which towed heavy and formidable-looking weapons. Everything was painted in khaki, a harsh attempt to recreate the natural camouflage that was so effortlessly displayed by the cygnets that were now living a less than peaceful existence up on the Mill Lake. For a village where the sight of even one motor car was regarded as unusual and a talking point, this was a stellar change in everybody's lives and routines. Soldiers were absolutely everywhere and each and every one of them, it seemed, had a bicycle to get around on. Village life, once calm, considered and thoroughly unhurried, became busy and eventful.

Take, for example, the three public houses that surrounded the village green. Before the arrival of the soldiers, the largest would very often close early in the evening owing to a lack of customers. But things were different now. At weekends, if someone fancied a quiet ale of an evening, they might find themselves unable to get into the Crown or the Green Man as they would be so full of soldiers, busily drinking and carousing the night away.

The British Legion did particularly well at this time, even sporting that rarest of things, a television set, which they procured in time for their eager patrons to watch a televised boxing match featuring Bruce Woodcock[4]: an event that would have been very well received by the Canadians who were probably eager for any sort of excitement. All of this sudden and very frenzied activity would, of course, have almost changed the lives of those pub landlords overnight for, after three or four years of being in the doldrums and eking out a very modest existence, they now didn't really know quite what had hit them and, more often than not, found themselves running out of beer and cigarettes. This, of course, was just the sort of situation that the village black market racketeer (and regardless what you might think of them, every community had to have one) would have thrived on. Such men were able, often at very short notice, to be able to produce the odd barrel of beer for a desperate landlord, else petrol (which was severely rationed) or just about anything else you needed – for the right price. Our own likeable racketeer was eventually called up before the beak (local magistrate) and asked if he wouldn't mind explaining his passion for red petrol, which was supplied to registered and official users only. When he was unable to provide a satisfactory answer, he was fined £50, a considerable sum when you consider that a working man's pay at the time was less than £3 a week.

Such a large fine might well have put some people off from such nefarious deeds. But not our man. Soon after that he was flogging silk stockings as well as rice which he'd bought from the Canadian soldiers.

Being situated in an area that relied a lot upon horses and agriculture, there was also a blacksmith's shop in the village, on the main street opposite the bus stop and public telephone box. We'd sometimes go into the blacksmith's shop to pump the arm of the bellows to ensure that his

---

4 Woodcock was a British light heavyweight and heavyweight boxer from Doncaster. The televised fight that the author is referring to may have been his win over Canadian champion Al Delaney in October 1944.

fire was kept burning bright and hot, especially when he was shoeing horses. The telephone box, resplendent with the crown of King George V attached to its roof was, like so many other places in Horsted Keyes, seldom frequented before the arrival of the Canadian soldiers. Now, however, following their transatlantic 'invasion', it would attract queues of soldiers on a nightly basis, all of whom were keen to impart their news to the folks back home. Sometimes that queue was so long, it would merge into the queue at the adjacent bus stop which would see people waiting for services to take them to Haywards Heath and Brighton, the town where I was born. You wouldn't often find we children queuing up for the bus unless we were off to school, but we did take a more than healthy interest in the phone box where, it was discovered, if you pressed button B, there would often be a happy dividend in the form of a couple of pennies, an occasional sixpence or even a shilling, something that would convert a hopeful gaze into a huge smile. And no wonder. As kids, we had never been so wealthy. But there was more than that to be found in the telephone box.

It wasn't that unusual to find a half-empty packet of cigarettes, a brand like Sweet Caporal, Craven A or even the odd Weights and Woodbine paper packet with one or two left from the five provided on the floor of the kiosk. These things were more than likely to have been left behind by the Canadians and didn't go to waste even though very few villagers smoked actual cigarettes, preferring, like my father, to roll their own. If I came home with some cigarettes for him, he'd break them into two pieces and mix the tobacco in with his Bruno pipe tobacco, a potent mix that used to stink the place to high heaven. This actually worked in my favour in the long run as it put me off smoking so much, I never took up the nasty habit and, from all the money that I saved, I eventually bought a house instead!

We'd all get so excited about the possibilities that existed within that telephone box that, more often than not, we'd end up, on school mornings, getting to the bus stop early so we could be the first people of the day to press the magic button B whilst, at the same time, searching the local area for any coins that the Canadians might have dropped. Our yield would normally depend on how many of them had used the phone box the night before and what state of inebriation they were in when they did so. My biggest find at this time was half a crown (equivalent to two shillings and sixpence), a discovery which made me, suddenly and quite unexpectedly, rather rich! Other money-making pastimes we'd engage in at the time (and you could never accuse any of us of not having an entrepreneurial spirit, despite our tender years) included collecting stray beer bottles and returning them to the pub in exchange for a few pennies. We certainly made the most of this one as, if the landlord of the Crown had forgotten to lock his back gate, some of those bottles would be 'recycled' time and time again.

Of all the camps that the Canadians set up in that once quiet and peaceful spot, the largest was situated around the Swimming Lake. Everywhere you looked around there, all manner of hitherto unseen contraptions were springing up or being developed for what they called their 'war games', with even a few tree houses being built high in the branches of the huge oaks. It was all fascinating to watch for us kids, especially when the soldiers were on the firing range. It wasn't unknown, especially if they wanted a little bit of peace and quiet later on, for the soldiers on the range to invite us to 'have a go' ourselves – which was easier said than done. At just nine years of age and standing knee-high to the proverbial grasshopper, I found it difficult enough to even lift the rifle, let alone hit the target whilst in the prone position. However, with a patient and worldly-wise French Canadian alongside me, helping to load and aim the rifle, improvement followed.

The rifle we were firing was the inevitable Lee Enfield .303, a weapon I became very familiar with later on in my life as I used it whilst shooting for the Pompey Command and the Far East fleet in Singapore – at least when I could be spared.

The Swimming Lake was used for its intended purpose with the Canadian soldiers regularly taking to its deep waters. In the middle of the lake, they erected a three-storey diving board that floated on four 45-gallon oil drums. This was only ever a temporary fix though and, after a while, they built a new and very stable diving board made of heavy wood which was about four feet wide by 50 feet long. Near to the lake's edge were two changing rooms, each built of corrugated iron.

The female one was situated deep in the trees and we used to climb on top of that and lie in wait on the roof, ready to spy on any unsuspecting lady bather below. Unfortunately, those corrugated panels used to make quite a lot of noise as we wriggled about and tried to get the best possible viewing position. These would have been sounds that were, at first, bewildering to the ladies below us who would reassure themselves by saying, 'Oh, it must be the wind,' only for the more alert amongst their number to point out that there wasn't any wind. This was at the time when we sussed out, through experience, that the effects of gravity can lead to you being hurt when you fall and land on hard sandstone. The resultant shock and pain hardly helped our attempts to flee the scene of the crime. There would always be some irate and barely clad females leading the way; they would alternate shouting at us with requests for the assistance of PC Franks who, as was his uncanny gift, never seemed to be too far away.

The largest of these three lakes might have been known as the Swimming Lake. But it wasn't as if any of us were competent swimmers at the time. We could manage a sort of 'doggy paddle' which would come in handy when you were belting off the edge of the diving board as fast as possible on a bike, as you could, at least, manage to splash and splutter your way to the bank. The next task, of course, would be to retrieve the bike from the bottom of the lake which meant holding your nose, going under and searching the water for the bike – and making sure you came back up again with the right one.

Now this was done in water that was only around ten feet deep, but, combined with the fact that the soldiers ended up teaching us how to swim properly, it was a good experience for us all in giving us confidence in the water. It certainly helped me in later years as I was known for being able to swim two lengths of a swimming pool underwater.

The track leading to the swimming pool was made up of clinkers that had been raked out of the boilers from the St Martin's jam factory, which was owned by the same Johnny Clark whose land all the soldiers were now camped on. During particularly dry periods, clouds of dust from those paths used to fly into the air when we raced each other down towards the lake on our bicycles. On one such day I was racing away in front of several other boys, happily showing off my new 'hand-made' bike which I had put together using two different wheels, a broken saddle, twisted handlebars and assorted other odds and ends – not forgetting, of course, a rusty but working bell which PC Franks insisted upon. It didn't matter what the bike looked like or how unlikely a contraption it was, just as long as it had a bell on it, he'd then be happy.

So content was I in my rapid descent down the path that I ended up flying over the edge of the bank and into the lake, an unintentional splashdown with my bike on this occasion, and one that took me several feet out of my depth and desperately dog paddling back to the bank, swallowing what seemed like a few gallons of murky water as I did so. My mates eventually caught up and managed to get me out of the water, just in time as, by then, my world was spinning around in front of me: their faces, the bikes, the trees, everything. In addition to that, my right arm had been heavily grazed and was now covered in a gory potpourri of clinker and blood. Worse of all, my nice clean shirt which less than an hour ago had been fresh, ironed and pristine was very much the worse for wear.

My immediate thoughts were therefore not about my own injuries or the damage that might have been inflicted upon my bike but about what Mum was going to say – or, worse, do – when she saw me. Fortunately, I came out of it relatively unscathed. Mother had, I guess, seen the state I was in and had decided that the fright I'd had was sufficient punishment for me. Yet, later that same day, as I was inspecting what was left of my bike, one of the soldiers explained that I had probably pedalled backwards and, in the process, flipped off it and into the water. This was my initiation into the mysteries of the back-pedalling braking system, which, before this particular incident, I had never been aware of. Well, I was now.

It may seem that my life at the time was one giant bundle of fun and games centred around our transatlantic guests. But this was not the case, and I had lots of other things to do to keep me occupied. One of my other pastimes during the war years, for example, was rearing Aylesbury ducks in our back garden. I used to buy them as chicks from a Miss Field who lived opposite a magnificent display of rhododendrons on the corner of a road that led to Dane Hill, affectionately referred to locally as Friends Corner. It was an absolutely stunning display of foliage and colour that I used to admire every year. I was more than surprised to discover, years later, when I was in an aircraft flying from Bangkok to Chiang Mai in Thailand, to see thick smoke billowing up towards us, the result of huge fires that are lit all over Thailand where this attractive shrub is treated as a creeping and poisonous parasite. Back home, the plant was a reminder that I was near Miss Field's home, and they proliferated year by year into a quite magnificent and undisturbed display. In addition to the ducks, I also reared chickens and rabbits which helped to sustain our need for good meat during those troubled times when many of the basics were strictly rationed.

Such diligence and an awareness, even at a young age, that I could not spend all of my time playing with my friends helped a great deal and, compared to many, our family lived fairly well during the war years. I also attended school of course, although that part of my young life wasn't as carefree as the rest of it, as I invariably found myself placed in the 'in-between' classes. This meant my education was constantly disturbed as social services saw fit to shunt me from one Sussex school to another. This was necessary, apparently, because my mother, alone because Father was working in London (his job being to clear the debris resulting from the Luftwaffe's bombing raids) was finding it difficult to handle me and my four young sisters on her own, something that I most certainly would not have agreed with. But then my choice or thoughts in the matter counted for nothing and, whenever I dared to voice an opinion, I was usually told to run along and play somewhere.

Maybe all that uncertainty is what made me feel so comfortable and reassured whenever we were amongst the Canadian soldiers, kindly men who would always give the time of day to a curious child such as me. Yet, later on in that summer of 1944, the soldiers suddenly upped and left the village. This not only left many of the eligible young women in the area nothing less than distraught, but also upset everyone else who had become used to their presence, not least the pub landlords who, after a period of prosperity, suddenly found their bars empty again. As for those young and extremely kind-hearted soldiers, many of them never had the good fortune to make it back to Canada; dozens ended up not even making it onto Juno beach in Normandy on D-Day. But it was not quite all doom and gloom in their wake for at least two of the young ladies from our village were claimed after the war and ended up making new lives for themselves in Canada. It was quite an extraordinary time for all of us and I often think of those Canadian soldiers who brought a little life into our village that summer, and who collectively gave so very much to us without asking for, or getting, anything in return.

Towards the end of the war, and with the village more or less back to its quiet and relatively untroubled pre-war ways, my father commenced work as a welder, working on the secret PLUTO (Pipe Line Under The Ocean) project which ended up supplying fuel to the allies in Europe after D-Day, June 4th 1944. This was very much a 'cloak and dagger' operation which necessitated the pump stations on the southern coast of England to be disguised as buildings that would afford no more than a second glance – including from enemy spies. They were therefore disguised to look like workers' cottages and garages. Some of them survive to this day, including the aptly named Pluto Cottage which is in Dungeness and is now a successful bed-and-breakfast business.

My father had certainly got himself involved in a very ingenious plan, one that was intended to support Allied troops in France after the invasions of D-Day. Liquid fuel from storage depots in England would be moved across the country via a more traditional pipeline to locations on the south coast (including what is now Pluto Cottage) before the pipeline continued, via the bottom of the English Channel, to France. It was one of those wonderfully risky yet bordering on genius decisions that war seems to provoke in people; technically very complex, of course, but also one that would negate the need to send large petrol and oil tankers to France at the time of the invasion as these would, of course, be inviting targets for the German Navy as well as the Luftwaffe.

And it gained the approval of the great American general and future US president Dwight D. Eisenhower, who said of PLUTO that it was, in his opinion, 'second in daring only to the Mulberry Harbours'. Praise indeed.

So that was the Second World War, a daring underwater project and my father. But what about me?

Well, my life had to change after all that had been happening and what I had seen and experienced as a result of that war. I was still only eleven years old at the time of PLUTO and D-Day. But I'd seen the pictures and read the stories that were printed in newspapers like the *Daily Herald* and *Daily Mirror;* the accounts of bravery and pictures depicting the brave men and ships that served the Allied cause so nobly throughout the war. I'd seen the air-to-air combat in the blue skies above the lanes and fields near to our home, had witnessed the wreckage of aircraft and the lifeless bodies of the men who had flown them and died with them. I'd also grown used to the companionship and camaraderie of the Canadian soldiers, men who had travelled to a foreign land in order to train to fight an enemy that they barely knew. Indeed, some of them probably didn't even know where Germany was prior to the war breaking out. Yet, there they were, thousands of miles from home and befriending the likes of me, many of them knowing that they probably wouldn't see home again but all too willing to fight and die for a just cause.

It's the sort of thing that can't help but have a major impact on a child's life. And it most certainly did mine, paving the way for a journey that went onto take up much of my adult life. From then on, despite my still tender years, there was never going to be any doubt.

I was going to join the Royal Navy.

CHAPTER 2

A Boy Sailor

'The Royal Navy recruiting officer who I saw was a heavily built, bearded and extremely weather-beaten chief petty officer who had rows of medal ribbons strewn across his left chest. He soon put me at my ease by recalling some of the events involving the Royal Navy which had taken place during the war before, and with all the force of a battleship fusillade, he started to question me, each query followed by another in a succession of demands that seemed endless.'

My first experience of life aboard ship came in 1946. I was thirteen and, on leaving school, joined the TS (training ship) *Arethusa*, known to all and sundry as the *'Arry*. This was a four-masted steel barque[1] that had originally been built and launched in Germany. The tallest mast topped out at around 185 feet which, believe me, if you're even near to the top of it, is quite a dizzying height. One of the ship's original routes had been as a merchant ship for the nitrate trade between Germany and Chile. This meant regular journeys around Cape Horn, widely reputed as the toughest expanse of water in the world to sail and navigate – something I am more than happy to confirm. Life now was slightly more gentle as the ship took on board the sailors of the future, me and the 239 other boys who'd joined with me. None of us were known by our names; we were all given numbers, with mine being 173. I was also allocated a division which was *forecastle* (the forward part of a ship just below the deck) *port, number four mess* – the first of many more to come. There were eight boys to each mess with our sleeping needs taken care of, just

---

1 A sailing ship, typically with three masts.

as they would have been in Lord Nelson's day, by hammocks that were slung over the tables in the mess. Any new boys that joined the mess were automatically referred to as 'nozzers' and had to join the mess at the bottom of the table. Once a boy had reached the top of his table, and this normally took around two years, it meant he was now considered ready and able to choose and embark upon his chosen professional career in either the Royal Navy or the Merchant Navy.

The education we had on board *Arethusa* was split between schooling in the general subjects, for example, mathematics and English, plus more specific discipline relating to the work that we would end up doing: making and mending our clothing; basic seamanship; boat work; knots and splices; navigation and communications systems. The latter included Morse code, flags and semaphore, so there was very much a tendency to get us living and breathing in naval mode as quickly as possible. Nothing beats that sort of schooling at an early age and we got it. Discipline was fairly strict, just as it would need to be on board ship. Boys who were found smoking were dealt with harshly with six cuts of the cane, often within minutes of being caught. A search of both the guilty boy's locker and those of his messmates would follow. Something else which was very much frowned upon was insubordination. You only needed to show it once, there were no second chances. Three cuts the first time and, for every subsequent misdemeanour, there would be an increase on that. Even perceived lesser offences, such as digging the pitch from between the wooden planks so you could chew on it, would merit some kind of punishment, although it wouldn't have been quite as severe as being caned.

I wouldn't want anyone thinking that I was a 'model sailor' during my time on the *Arethusa*. I fell foul of the first lieutenant, aka 'Jimmy the One' or just plain Jimmy, on a couple of occasions – which wasn't that difficult to do. On the first occasion I was one of several boys who had been caught in the new heads (lavatories) and accused of smoking, something which I was most definitely not guilty of doing. No protestations of innocence were being entertained, however, and we were all, as one, herded into the gym ready to receive six cuts of the cane each, strokes that would be applied as we all, one by one, bent down over a gym horse. I didn't want to be whacked with a thin cane on my bare bum for something that I hadn't done so I promptly ran out of there, barefoot and dressed in only a pair of blue shorts and my underpants, up onto the upper deck which was covered in snow. I was aware that I was being pursued so didn't stop there, but instead made a bee-line for the mainmast which we were required to climb from time to time, that mast which soared to a height almost 20 feet taller than Nelson's Column. Fortunately, heights never bothered me and never have. I'd already climbed this particular mast several times before, right up to the final six feet under the 'truck' or 'button', that tiny area of space the button boy has to stand on at the thrilling conclusion of the famous naval ceremony that was once familiar to so many people. As I climbed, my pursuers followed, first up and over the devil's elbow where the yardarms joined and then up and over the second devil's elbow before climbing to the very top, hugging the mast underneath the button.

It was very cold although I didn't feel it at that time. All I wanted, all I cared about was being listened to by someone who would believe me when I said that I hadn't been smoking. I eventually came down after Captain Campbell, who had left the sanctuary of his cabin in order to find out what all the fuss had been about, promised that no harm would come to me for my actions. Inevitably, my icy climb to the top of the mast meant I ended up in the ship's sick bay where I stayed for some time, along with four other boys. After three days or so, we all became very aware of the frequent visits that 'Jimmy the One' was making to the sick bay office in order to spend time with the matron. I didn't put two and two together myself but the buzz soon got around the ship that the first lieutenant was having an affair with the matron. Word of this soon reached Jimmy's ears, but he had an easy excuse of course, choosing to apportion the blame for the 'rumour' on we boys who had been in the sick bay at the time.

The other occasion that saw me fall under the baleful eye and actions of Jimmy was when, shortly after I'd been discharged from sick bay back into my mess, he caught me chewing some pitch which I'd scraped from between the wooden planks of the upper deck. My punishment for this was being made to stand to attention on the quarter deck, which, fortunately, was under cover. And I say that because it was February at the time and a bitter east wind, mixed with snow, was blowing. This didn't stop Jimmy from picking out two of us who, after such a long time standing around, had resorted to fidgeting. He picked me and one other boy out of the comparative calm of the quarter deck and, clad again in just our underpants and blue shorts, we were made to stand underneath both of the tall wind scoops on the upper deck which our First Lieutenant had turned around purposefully in order that we'd be fully exposed to that biting east coast wind. The outcome of this, hardly a surprising one, is that I ended up in sick bay again and became extremely unwell. This time it was serious and I became so ill, I had to be transferred to St Bartholomew's Hospital in Rochester where I stayed for several weeks before being discharged from both the hospital and the *Arethusa* because, it was said, I had a 'suspected tubercular gland'. This was, as I later learnt, a roundabout way of saying I had tuberculosis which, of course, was most emphatically not the case.

Jimmy was quite the character. One of the regular jobs we boys on the *'Arry* had was to climb the hill opposite the ship to work in either his garden or his house. I only went into the house on one occasion but can still vividly remember the mantelpiece in his living room where nude photographs of himself, his wife and several other people were prominently displayed. The boys who were in the house more regularly than me had clearly heard or seen some things as they regularly spoke of 'goings-on' committed by both the first lieutenant and his wife. I am sure that, if such things were to happen and be made public today, the media would have the ultimate field day and, maybe even back then, they would have done if the truth about what really went on 'behind closed doors' on *Arethusa* had ever been revealed. But it never got out and, over time, both facts and people's memories distort and fade. Fortunately for me, I was never subject to anything much more shocking than the realisation Jimmy had these photographs on public display in his living room.

Yet, despite all the bad experiences that I'd already had, not least those at the hands of the infamous Jimmy, my mind was set upon joining the Royal Navy. I'd read the *Daily Mirror* every day during the war and, prior to it being torn up for use as toilet paper, had been enthralled at the exploits of the ships and the brave men of the Royal Navy who had sailed them. Then, from the dizzying heights of *Arethusa*'s masts, I, along with all the other boys, had watched the warships returning from the war, often with serious and very visible damage, all destined for Chatham dockyard. And believe me, some of the damage they'd incurred was horrendous. But it acted only to harden my resolve. I was going to join the Royal Navy, come what may.

***

Three years later I made good that promise to myself by applying to join the Royal Navy at their recruiting office in Brighton. But, confident as I was of my desire, my nerves were on edge as I was worried that the letter confirming my interview with them would be intercepted by my mother (who was dead set against me joining any of the armed services) and that would be the end of that, certainly as far as she was concerned. But luck was on my side: that eagerly awaited letter arrived whilst I was working in the garden and could take it from the postman myself. Having got over that particular obstacle, however, I then had another one to concern me as the day of my interview grew ever closer: I was hoping and praying that my time on the *Arethusa* and consequent departure for (spurious) 'medical reasons' wouldn't be mentioned as that would almost certainly have disqualified me from being able to even apply, such were the Navy's strict entry criteria, even then. It was a thought that just wouldn't go away, and yet, for all that, when I arrived in Brighton and caught my first sight of the sea from the top of the hill that Brighton station stands upon, I had a distinctly happy flutter in my heart. I'd only seen the sea once before in my entire life but, at that time, the beach had been shrouded with barbed wire and armed soldiers whose duty was to keep an eye on those coastal waters at all times, such was the fear of an attempted invasion on our shores from Nazi Germany.

That war had now been over for nearly four years and normality was, slowly but surely, beginning to return to everyday life. Roadside stanchions that had, for some five years or more, been devoid of their signposts were once again displaying place names and the distances needed to travel to get to them. These had all been removed in September

1939 in order to make life for any invading army as difficult as possible, something that it would, doubtless, have achieved. It made life rather tedious and time consuming for the local population as well, but that was a small price to pay. I could now stand in Brighton and know exactly where places like London, Hove, Worthing and Eastbourne were and what direction and distance from that venerable old seaside town they were. It was a small but hugely significant change that must have meant a great deal to many people, especially those locals who had perhaps ended up getting as lost as any enemy soldier might have done as a result of their temporary removal.

The Royal Navy recruiting officer who I saw was a heavily built, bearded and extremely weather-beaten chief petty officer who had rows of medal ribbons strewn across the left side of his chest. He soon put me at my ease by recalling some of the events involving the Royal Navy which had taken place during the war before, and with all the force of a battleship fusillade, he started to question me, each query followed by another in a succession of demands that seemed endless.

'Why do you want to join the Royal Navy?'

'Have any of your family served in the Navy?'

'Have you ever been at sea?'

'What kind of work have you been doing since you left school?'

Tough it might have been, but I was prepared and gave what I considered to be good answers to all of his questions. He then took me through, step by step, each of the various branches of occupation that might have been open to me: seaman, engine room, cook, steward, fleet air arm, communications and medical, for example, before going onto explain that the seaman branch was split into many different specialities. There were, for example, diver, radar, navigation and ASDIC, which was an early form of sonar that was used to detect enemy submarines. Endless options that invited question after question after question, and perhaps amidst all this glorious and seemingly infinite detail I should have been confused, lost in a world that I couldn't even begin to understand.

Except that I wasn't.

'My ambition is to be a wireless operator.' I said it with confidence and with as much conviction as I could give.

'Telegraphist?' he interjected.

'Yes,' I hastily replied, 'I want to be a telegraphist.'

An air of gloom and silence now enveloped the office. The chief petty officer was alternating between looking at me and the papers he had in front of him. When he spoke, they were words I didn't want to hear.

'Your school qualifications count you out for the communications branch to be a telegraphist, I'm afraid. To be brutally honest, you haven't got any qualifications at all, have you? Mind you, judging by the number of schools you have been to, passed from one to another due to the war, your lack of qualifications is hardly one of your own making.'

By now I was waiting with some trepidation for a mention of the *Arethusa*. None came.

'If I were you,' he went on, 'I would think about joining the seaman branch and sub-specialising later. Firstly, and most importantly, you have to pass the first six weeks of basic training. That is, of course, providing you pass your medical examination which we will do here today. If that is successful, you will be sent to HMS *St Vincent* at Gosport, Portsmouth, later this year. We will, of course, require your parents' signature.' With that, he handed me the necessary papers. My surprise at hearing those words must surely have been noticed. I went on to have my medical and, having passed that, and with no mention whatsoever of my time on *Arethusa* being made, the train journey home was one of complete bliss. My only nagging worry was what my mother would say when she found out what I'd done because, even though I had now, to all intents and purposes, fulfilled my dream and joined the Royal Navy, I still needed her to give formal permission for me to do so.

It wasn't as if I could tell my father first and ask him to sign the papers. He'd been away from home for long periods of time helping to clear the damage that had been done to London during the Blitz before commencing his work on the PLUTO project. So it was up to Mother to sign the papers. I got it done eventually but only after countless attempts through forging her signature.

Funnily enough, one of the first things I'd done after I got home from the interview was not to find Mother but to get out my old school atlas so I could look at the map of Great Britain in order to ascertain exactly where Portsmouth was! At least that meant I knew where I was going and, what's more, I could get to Portsmouth from Haywards Heath on the train quite quickly. I still couldn't bring myself to tell my mother what I was doing, though and, when the day came to leave home and join the Royal Navy, I left whilst she was at work, leaving her a letter explaining what I had done, knowing that, in time, she would forgive me. Any fears about leaving home, if indeed there were any at all, were soon quashed by the feeling of pride when I produced my railway warrant at Haywards Heath station in exchange for a train ticket to Portsmouth, a thrill that remains with me to this day. I had, along with my warrant, an accompanying letter explaining how to join the naval ferry at Portsmouth Harbour, a short walk from the station, which would take me over the short stretch of water to Gosport and the training base the Royal Navy had set up for boys and juniors on HMS *St Vincent*. This information was all written down on what was, for me, a very special piece of headed paper that I kept hold of for a very long time afterwards.

No wonder that piece of paper was so precious. It was confirmation that, finally, I had achieved my aim. I was now officially 'on board' as a recruit and had become a Boy Seaman, Second Class – as low down the ranks as you could possibly get in the Royal Navy. I was full of hope for what my future might hold but even in my wildest and most ambitious of dreams I wouldn't have seen myself, as was the case, eventually holding the rank of master-at-arms, the highest possible non-commissioned rank in the Royal Navy – and closing *St Vincent* down, something I, sadly, was involved with later on in my naval career.

HMS *St Vincent* had been opened in 1927 primarily as a shore establishment, with a short interruption during the war when, amongst other things, it was home to the Navy's torpedo section. At the end of the war it was pressed back into action as a training base and now, four years on, was welcoming me and the other young hopefuls, all boys, who wanted to join the service. Although I was still relieved that it hadn't been mentioned at my interview, my experience as a one-time training ship boy on HMS *Arethusa* helped me immensely through the tough first six-week period of square bashing at HMS *St Vincent*. In fact, contrary to the experiences of a few of my peers, I ended up quite enjoying it. There were, inevitably, a number of boys who dropped out for one reason or another, two of the main causes being homesickness and bed wetting. After what seemed like an eternity, those six weeks of doing little else but marching all over the parade ground came to an end one sunny Friday afternoon. For some it would, sadly, also mean the end of their naval careers for it was at that point that decisions would be made about the future prospects of each and every boy in my class, including, of course, myself. Would I be staying on or would I be out? I'd temporarily cheered myself up once we'd finished for the day by regarding the sunny weather as being a good omen, but optimism was soon tempered when the rumour went around that at least two of the boys now sitting with me in the main hall waiting for the training commander's verdict had failed.

Was I one of them? The tension was unbearable.

Our class was the third to have its results read out. We had, in listening to the verdicts given on the boys that made up the first two classes, already witnessed disappointments as well as some elements of surprise. Now, the boys in our class, sat upon the highly polished floor of the main hall at HMS *St Vincent,* were so het up with nerves and frustration that we began to collectively fidget, looking for all the world as if we were suffering from St Vitus Dance – a perhaps understandable response to the tension that drew shouts and implied threats from he who must be obeyed, the chief petty officer, a reaction which only heightened the state of extreme apprehension.

As I have already written, the branch of the Royal Navy I wanted to join had been in communications so I could train to be a telegraphist, that is, an operator who used a telegraph key to send and receive Morse code in order to communicate between ships or from ship to shore. It was one of the first professions within the service which might now be regarded as somewhat 'hi tech', at least for its time. This is why that chief petty officer at the recruitment centre in Brighton had told me that my lack of a proper education made me unsuitable for such a role. In other words, he, on behalf of the Royal Navy, had looked through my papers and decided that I wasn't bright enough for such a relatively new and demanding role. But, rather than diminish my hopes, the way that he'd pretty much written off my chances of ever becoming a telegraphist had made me even more determined than ever to do so. Why? Because that particular branch was considered to be the 'crème de la crème' of the Royal Navy. For me, if I was going to be serving with the best then why not be part of the very best of the best? The Royal Navy depended upon swift and efficient communications; indeed, in a rapidly modernising Navy, effective communication was pretty much everything. This meant that a lot of the boy sailors I was alternately working alongside or competing against wanted to take up communications as well. So it was always going to be tough for me. But my resolve and determination never wavered.

But right now, sat waiting on that hard wooden floor at HMS *St Vincent*, I just wanted to know if I'd passed or not. And the lieutenant commander was about to put us all out of our misery.

'Of the twenty-four boys who started the course, we are left with just fifteen and, of these, Boy Seaman Second Class…'

My heart felt as if it had stopped as a deadly hush swept over us. Faces dropped, breathing became heavier. In everyone's mind, the same question was now being asked: who is going to be sent home?

'Regretfully…' the lieutenant commander said, before pausing and repeating himself; this was becoming unbearable. 'Regretfully, Boy Second Class Bowden, your class leader, has been kept in Haslar hospital where he has a fractured ankle so he will not be progressing onwards to HMS *Ganges* as planned. All of the other boys in this class, however, have passed. Some, I might add, have done so by the skin of their teeth but they have scraped through. Twelve will be going to HMS *Ganges* to start the intense communication course.'

Was I one of them? I knew the odds had been against me right from the start, given that interview, but I had given everything I could during those six weeks. The lieutenant commander then continued.

'Names of all those selected are already displayed on the main notice board. A replacement for Boy Bowden is yet to be decided. Boys who will not be going on to HMS *Ganges* for the communication course will be classed up with the others and commence the seamanship course due to start here on Monday.'

I didn't hear anything after that. I wasn't aware of the chief petty officer ordering us to dismiss or all the other boys getting up and leaving the hall. I was certain that my name wasn't on that board so I just sat there, disappointed beyond belief that I wouldn't, after all, be training in Communications. It had been a long shot, of course it had and it wasn't as if the Navy hadn't made that clear. But, even so, it felt, at that moment, as if my world had ended.

Jimmy James, one of the boys who I'd palled up with, soon brought me back into the land of the living. Grabbing my arm, he said, 'Come on Tone, let's get a cuppa in the NAAFI.' The first sip of that tea brought me back to my senses and we discussed who we thought would be going off to do communications at HMS *Ganges* in place of the injured Ginger Bowden. Jimmy was one of those going, having already been told and, in the faint hope that my name was, after all, on the list, we made a bee-line for the main noticeboard in the canteen flat which, for some reason, seemed deathly quiet all of a sudden and rather eerie with it.

Not expecting a miracle, I read down the board.

'The following boys have been selected for the communications course at HMS *Ganges*. Baker, Barnes, Bowden, Cooper...' My interest waned; I didn't want to read any further. But Jimmy wasn't going to let me wallow in my disappointment. Putting his arm around my shoulder, he said, 'All's not lost Tone, Ginger's replacement has yet to be named.'

'Some hope my name will come up,' I managed to spit out, quietly sobbing as I did and hoping the others wouldn't see me.

'Come on, Tony,' he said. 'Let's finish our game of chess, the chief yeoman will let us know after supper what's going to happen.'

By now, I was beginning to pull myself together a little bit, reasoning that at least I'd be staying in the Navy and, with that, maybe opting to become a naval diver; that would be *much* better than being a telegraphist. Did I convince myself of that though? No, probably not. And, although I was now accepting the fact I'd have to look at an alternative career path within the Royal Navy, the disappointment at not being selected to train as a telegraphist was very acute indeed. I went back with Jimmy, we finished our game of chess which I lost, par for the course on that day I suppose, and, after that, we opted to go to the barrack cinema along with a few other class mates where *In Which We Serve* (starring Noel Coward and John Mills, amongst others) was being shown.

Saturday morning arrived with the usual cry of, 'Wakey wakey, rise and shine, the sun's blazing your eyeballs out.' I got up and, as I dressed and made my bed, I couldn't help but think that maybe there was still a chance I'd been selected to go on the telegraphist course in place of the unfortunate Ginger Bowden. All too quickly, however, my early morning reverie was disturbed by the strident voice of the chief yeoman.

'Daydreaming, are we, Beasley?' His not-so-dulcet tones cut through me like a dose of salts as he continued: 'I want to see you, after supper, in my mess room.'

'Yes chief. I mean sir,' I replied, fully expecting his standard retort about how he was no Red Indian and neither were his mother and father, so stop calling him 'chief'… but it never came, there was just silence accompanied by a grin from the chief petty officer who was with him.

Once supper was over, I made myself presentable. Sitting outside the chief petty officer's mess room, I'd noticed two other boys, Sharky Ward and Dodger Long. My heart duly switched frequency, increasing twenty to the dozen. Me, a telegraphist, what was I thinking? Clearly I was here, along with Sharky and Dodger, to find out what they were going to do with us. 'Wishful thinking,' I kept saying to myself. 'Wishful thinking.' At that moment, the chief yeoman's voice thundered down the entire length of the corridor.

'Long!' Dodger jumped up so swiftly that his chair went flying from underneath him, assisted in its transit by the highly polished deck. A couple of minutes later, I heard the room door to the parade ground close with a very definitive thud.

'Ward!' Sharky left his chair with considerably more care, ran his fingers through his hair and entered the room. After what seemed ages, he too left the mess room via the parade ground door rather than the one he'd entered by. Another thud. Another brief silence. I waited for my name to be called but it seemed as if it was never going to happen. Then the door opened and the chief yeoman came out and looked me up and down before saying, 'The last one, eh, Beasley? What are we going to do with you?'

That got me trembling. Maybe I was going to be thrown out after all?

'Close the door and sit down.' Was this man speaking to me, actually speaking to me in a normal manner rather than, as all the instructors tended to do, bawling his head off? I didn't quite know what to think. He continued, calm, still authoritative but almost friendly in his tone.

'I have spent a good half hour talking about you to the training officer. We parted agreeing to disagree, if you know what I mean. Lieutenant Commander Upton feels we will be wasting time and money sending you to HMS *Ganges* to do the communications course so that you may become a naval telegraphist. Your schooling, as you know, is abysmal; however, as I have argued, that is not all your fault. You are willing and there is no other suitable candidate available. You also have a good knowledge of Morse code, semaphore and flags, so I am willing to stick my neck out for you.'

Fortunately, he hadn't asked me where I had learned these communication skills, else I would have had to tell him about my time on *Arethusa* which might have put an end to my naval career there and then. I felt calm and just sat there in front of him without saying anything. It seemed as if I was waiting for hours for him to speak again but, when he did, the words were some of the most wonderful I had yet heard in my young life.

'Yes, you are going to HMS *Ganges* in Bowden's place. I am sure that you will do your best. Don't let me down, will you?'

'No, chief.'

He glared at me before opening the parade ground door, tapped me on the shoulder and said, 'Well done.' Surprised? I was over the moon! Jimmy was waiting for me to appear and, as if he knew, he slapped me on the back and said, 'We can still be friends at *Ganges* now.' I was, of course, beyond delighted to be moving on to the *Ganges* and to be training for the role that I had always wanted to do; but deep down, I knew that my selection had more to do with making up the numbers than anyone thinking I had a realistic chance of passing. Some people would take such a put-down to heart. For me, it was like a red rag to a bull. Lieutenant Commander Upton's conviction that I had little to no chance of passing the communications course was going to inspire me to work as hard as I could and prove both him and any other doubters wrong in the process.

CHAPTER 3

Early Days at Sea

'I now knew, in no uncertain terms, just how sacrosanct the Rum Fanny was aboard any ship. This fact was emphasised to me by the killick's actions in making me aware of the fact which resulted in my flying across the mess and ending up in the hammock netting amongst all of the mess hammocks. Further expletives were then offered, which I could only faintly hear in the background as there seemed to be a loud buzzing in my right ear where the killick had thumped me.'

A great many events took place in 1949. In Britain, the film *The Third Man*, an adaptation of Graham Greene's masterpiece, had been released and would go on to win that year's Grand Prix prize at the Cannes Film Festival; whilst in the former Nazi Germany, the Allied military authorities relinquished control of the nation's remaining assets to the new Federal Republic of Germany, to be led by Federal Chancellor Konrad Adenauer.

Things were livening up across the pond as well. President Harry S. Truman had commenced his first term that January and in the same month, the North Atlantic Treaty was signed in Washington, leading to the formation, of course, of NATO. June 1949 saw the last US troops stationed in South Korea return home whilst, for those of you fond of vintage television broadcasts, June also saw the start in the US of the very first TV Western series, namely *Hopalong Cassidy* on NBC.

Slightly closer to home, was a glorious new era of peace in mainland Europe on the horizon? Perhaps. Or perhaps not. Our potential new adversary, the Soviet Union, had vetoed United Nations membership for Ceylon (now Sri Lanka), Finland, Iceland, Italy, Jordan and Portugal.

Soviet sabre-rattling continued when President Truman announced that the Soviet Union had successfully tested its first atomic bomb.

I didn't know it at the time but, in the years to come, the Soviet Union was going to become a focal point of interest for the Royal Navy – and I was most definitely going to be part of that ongoing interest. But the only thing that mattered for a certain Tony Beasley in September 1949 was that he was going to join HMS *Ganges* at Shotley Gate near Ipswich in Suffolk. I was excited and, of course, very nervous about the prospect of what lay ahead. I had been sent along as a bit of a 'third man' myself, someone to make up the numbers due to the sporting misadventures of the unfortunate Bowden. Then there was Lieutenant Commander Upton back at HMS *St Vincent* who was convinced that my coming to *Ganges* was going to be a 'waste of time and money'. I wanted to prove him wrong. But, more than that, I wanted to pay back the trust and support that the Vincent's chief had shown in me and pass the course.

At least I was in familiar company. The twelve boys from HMS *St Vincent*, including my pal Jimmy James, had joined twelve from HMS *Ganges'* own intake. I'd got this opportunity, one that I was going to share in some good company. But the ball was now entirely in my court. Pass or fail, it was down to me and me alone.

HMS *Ganges* had opened as a boys' training establishment in October 1945, expanding its facilities and taking in ever increasing numbers of boys to train almost straight away. And no wonder. The Royal Navy had lost 50,758 men, all known to have been killed in action during the Second World War, with a further 820 reported as missing. Then there were 14,663 wounded in action. The Navy was woefully short of both men and ships and it was the role of establishments such as *Ganges* to train their replacements and have them ready to serve as soon as possible. This meant, for me and all the other intake on that bright September morning, twenty-six weeks that were split into two separate 'terms', which turned out to be very hard graft indeed. And, initially, I was able to keep pace with everyone, learning all the unusual and unique ways in which Morse code, semaphore and flags were used on a ship at sea as well as, inevitably, some basic parade-ground drill using .303 rifles. Then there was general seamanship and boat work, which played a more and more prominent role in our training as the days and weeks went by. It was all very intense and tremendously hard work. Mind you, with regard to the latter, the weather didn't help. Being situated on the east coast of England, *Ganges* was subject to some biting winds off the North Sea and the bitter weather that came with them. I found the cold almost unbearable and often ended up in trouble for wearing items of clothing that were otherwise forbidden.

Time passed quickly and, come mid-term, the halfway results were through – and I had passed. We'd been split into two groups known as Sparkers and Buntings. The Sparkers, myself included, were the budding wireless telegraphists who'd be busy working down below in nice warm offices whilst the Buntings, who were flag wavers responsible for sending signals by semaphore, flags and Aldis lamps (a visual signalling device for optical communication which typically used Morse code) would be spending all of their time on the steel deck of an open bridge of their ship whatever the prevailing conditions or weather might be.

The twenty-six weeks that followed were difficult and I soon began to realise that my lack of education was, finally, becoming something of a stumbling block. But I was determined to pass and not only for my sake, but to prove all of the doubters wrong. So I gave it absolutely everything I had until that extremely gruelling period eventually came to an end and, thankful that I had managed to stay the course, I joined everyone else mustered in the gym where, once again, and just as we had back at HMS *St Vincent*, we sat down and waited to hear what our fate would be.

I mentioned that I was grateful to have been able to stay the course. I was. Many of the boys had dropped out for one reason or another, some of them quite early on as well. Of the original twenty-four in our class, ten had gone, which meant that fourteen of us remained. We were now about to find out if it had all been worth it and whether or not we had been able to leap over the final hurdle and were about to be passed out and promoted to the dizzy rank of Boy Telegraphist or Signal Boy second class. Fortunately, there was little to no preamble and all fourteen of us were swiftly told that we had passed. I cannot, even now, begin to describe the feeling that overwhelmed me at that time; elated simply isn't a good enough word to describe how I felt. I was also extremely pleased to have proved myself and been able to put one over on all of the 'doubting Thomas' who had been convinced (and not been shy in telling me of the fact) that I'd never make it this far.

Thus, on October 10th 1950, I passed out as a Boy Telegraphist and left *Ganges* in order to join my first ship. When the lists denoting everyone's final destinations was finally pinned onto the notice board, I scanned down the list of names until I read, *Boy Telegraphist T. Beasley to HMS* Loch Lomond. Now it was real. I'd done it. I'd proved everyone wrong and had passed and, what's more, was now on my way to join my first ship. I was going to be at sea as a serving member of the Royal Navy.

I noted that, at the same time as I was reading the postings, so was one of our instructors. Plucking up the courage to do so, I asked him what kind of ship HMS *Loch Lomond* was and where it was stationed. The instructor's reply surprised me so much, you could have knocked me down with the proverbial feather.

'HMS *Loch Lomond*? Never heard of her, lad.' He was slurring his speech as usual, not that I should have been particularly surprised at that, as the instructor in question was well known for being half piddled most of the time. Undeterred, I sought out another instructor and asked him the same question. Luckily, he was able to tell me everything I needed to know. HMS *Loch Lomond* was, I learned, in Sliema Creek in Malta as part of the Navy's Mediterranean fleet. As for my mate Jimmy, he was destined to join HMS *Flamingo* which was operating out in the Persian Gulf. We had to go our separate ways then, but that's the way of things in the Navy: you can be the best of mates with someone before one of you is spirited off somewhere else and you never see them again. Happily, Jimmy and I were to stumble across one another again many years later in the Far East.

***

In a mix of excitement and trepidation at what might lie ahead, I flew out to Malta with others of my class in order to join the various ships we'd been posted to. Until now I had been amongst and training with boys of my own age; I'd now be joining a ship where, in all possibility, I'd be the youngest serving seaman on board. My mind was racing as I alighted from the transport and onto the jetty in the creek, looking out for my ship amongst all of those that were tied up there.

They all, I have to admit, looked pretty much the same to me. So put yourself in my shoes. I'm about to commence serving King and Country on board one of His Majesty's warships and I'm not entirely certain which one I should be boarding. Which one is it? I daren't ask. Fortunately, a motor cutter soon came alongside where some of us were standing, the coxswain in it shouting up to us, 'Who's for *Loch Lomond* then?' Saved! I threw my hammock and kitbag into the cutter and we were on our way. Within a few minutes, we came alongside F437 HMS *Loch Lomond*. My first ship.

'Up you go, lad,' said the chap in the cutter, adding, 'Leave your bag and hammock, we'll get it after the cutter has been hoisted.' I climbed up the bosun's ladder and set foot on *Loch Lomond*. By now, I was completely and utterly bewildered. One thing that I do remember is being told by the ship's quartermaster (a naval petty officer with particular

HMS *Loch Lomond* (courtesy http://www.naval.history.net)

responsibility for steering and signals) that, 'When you step on board one of His Majesty's Ships lad, you stand to attention and salute. Now, what's your name?'

I had arrived and was as proud as punch.

HMS *Loch Lomond* was one of 28 Loch-class frigates. The Loch was a class of anti-submarine frigate that was built for both the Royal Navy and its allies during the Second World War. The ships' design was, for the time, a very innovative one that had been based on the experiences gained in three years of naval combat during the Battle of the Atlantic – as war always seems to do, it had brought to the fore some significant technological advances. These were now part of my new ship's armoury. It was a relatively new ship that had been launched in 1944, going onto serve for 25 years in the Royal Navy before being broken up for scrap.

I served on HMS *Loch Lomond* for around seventeen months, sailing around the Mediterranean and Red Sea and visiting, during my time there, some really interesting places, many of which are still firmly imprinted on my memory. But, of course, I had to get used to life aboard ship first of all. One of my first experiences of what it would be like was when the killick (leading seaman) in the mess asked if anyone could make a clacker pastry, that is, a little bit of pastry that was coated with jam, not unlike a jam tart and, sometimes, some dried fruit. Sheepishly, yet wanting to feel as if I could make a contribution, I said that I could – whereupon I was immediately appointed as 'cook of the grot' (mess), which involved preparing the food and making the clacker as well as getting some custard and a type of gravy referred to as RBG, that is, Rich Brown Gravy. Once I'd done that, I had to take the end result to the galley before cooking it all up for collection at the appropriate time. This was known as canteen messing. Each month an amount of money was allocated to each mess with which they would buy their food.

However, there was always a problem at the end of the month when the money, invariably, ran out. It was at this time that my favourite dinner, and the one I, as the most junior member of the mess, had been seconded into making, became the order of the day. Then there was Pot mess. This, as it was called, was the easiest meal to turn out and one that took very little time to make as it involved throwing whatever was available at the time into a large pot, mixing it thoroughly, heating and serving. It may not, I admit, sound the nicest meal in the world but believe me, the surprise is in the eating, it really is very nice. So that would be lunch or supper in the mess sorted. Breakfast was different, having it was virtually unheard of and most blokes settled for a cup of tea and a fag.

The contrasts between the types of ship at sea can vary considerably. A 'big ship' would refer to something like an aircraft carrier or cruiser, the workings of which are completely different to that of a small ship (like HMS *Loch Lomond*) such as a destroyer, minesweeper or corvette. The personnel serving on the big ships are known as 'big ship's crew' whilst, surprise surprise, those serving on the smaller ships are referred to as 'small ship's crew'. However, once you were part of a small ship's crew, that was pretty much how it was going to be for you for the rest of your career. I was, throughout my time in the Royal Navy, part of a small ship's crew where life was entirely different from that the crews on the larger ships would experience. The crew on those would have the relative luxury of having their bread, cakes, rolls, clacker and other related treats baked and freshly available on a daily basis. Not so on a smaller ship; whilst mail, the one thing a matelot (sailor) looks forward to more than just about anything else, is always in short supply on a small ship. You can wait for days and days just for a mail call – and then never get anything in it anyway.

You're also at a bit of a disadvantage if you're posted onto a small ship if you are looking to advance up the ranks and take the requisite examinations in order to do so. It was quite often the case that some of the questions in these exams would relate to equipment that is not found on the smaller ships, or, as in many cases, has not even been heard of by the men who serve aboard them. Then there is the advantage of being a member of a large crew, which means you can be temporarily relieved of your day-to-day duties in order that you can 'go back to school' and get some studying done. This, of course, means you gain advancement a lot more quickly than your peers on the smaller ships. In addition, compassionate cases can be dealt with a lot more easily on larger ships as there are invariably options available for crew members to be sent home if required if serious family circumstances demand it. You can even find yourself serving on a larger ship if some suffer from sea sickness and the constant pitching and rolling the smaller ships experience is too much for you – larger ships are far more stable whilst you are at sea, making their occupants' lives a lot more bearable.

When you are at sea aboard a small ship it becomes inevitable that, from time to time, water will find its way onto the lowest levels, which are the mess decks. This can present an interesting situation when it comes to having a meal down there. When you are away at sea for any prolonged period of time, you tend to store tins in the lockers at deck level. Our staple diet was therefore anything that you could get in a tin: meat, fruits, rice, curry, custard, chicken, turkey etc. The problem with water getting onto the deck, especially if it finds its way into the lockers, is that the labels on the tins will first become detached and then go 'walkabout'. That leaves you, the hungry sailor, with an array of tins that hold absolutely no clue as to what might be inside. To a certain extent, you can make a reasonable guess as to what the contents might be but, more often than not, opening one is a culinary stab in the dark, especially if it comes after 'tot' time, this being the naval reference to the distribution of the daily ration of rum.

To prevent any potential embarrassment to both myself and my messmates, I decided to use the situation in hand to cook up a very unique pot mess. This involved blindly selecting a tin, cutting the top off without looking before pouring its entire contents into a large cooking pot known as a mess fanny. I would repeat until the final tin had been emptied; give the still unknown contents a good old stirring to ensure that all the lumpy bits were being broken up and mixed together – pears, peaches, dumplings, tomatoes, onions etc – before placing the lid on and taking the whole thing to the galley for the chef to do his bit. Pot mess a'la Beasley. Taking the tops off the tins without looking sometimes resulted in my lacerating my fingers and it's probably fair to say the Beasley DNA ended up being scattered around a few of my ship mates in much the same way as it is generously distributed around the clematis and all the other active plants and vegetables that are in my garden today.

My own mess was in the fore ends, that is, the bow of the ship where the majority of the communications ratings, totalling 24 men, lived and slept. In those days, you slept in a hammock and, contrary to popular belief, a hammock is far superior to a bunk for several reasons, the main one being that you get a far better night's sleep, especially when the ship is heading into a force nine gale! One's hammock is a very personal and versatile space for any matelot who is also able to use it in order to stow away items like books, letters, money, photographs and duty frees. It may, I suppose, have made sense to have all of us communications specialists bedded down in the one area in order that we all got to know everyone else and became a very tight-knit team; but on the other hand, I often used to query the wisdom of putting us, or any specialists, into one place. A lesson should have been learnt when the battle-class destroyer HMS *Hogue* collided with the Indian cruiser *Mysore*, the incident resulting in *Hogue's* bow being completely destroyed. One rating was killed and three others wounded. That was bad enough, but, had the collision been much heavier or direct, the casualties might have been into double figures and, had it happened to our ship, nearly all of the communications specialists might have been wiped out in an instant.

As cook of the mess, I was also responsible for its cleanliness. Any gear that was left sculling about the place was put into the 'scan bag' with a small fee due to be paid for its retrieval when the guilty party came to collect it, a fund which we were eventually able to use to replace any utensils and similar items that might have been lost. Anything not claimed after what was deemed to be a reasonable time was then subjected to the dreaded float test, that is, it was thrown overboard. Use it or lose it, that was my mantra and I stuck to it.

Looking after the mess on any ship is a far more onerous duty than you might suppose. Take, for example, items such as cups, saucers, knives, forks and spoons. Each member of the mess would have one allocated to him and, if something was broken or lost, it had to be paid for. Cutlery was not breakable of course but it was the sort of item that was lost the most, mainly as the men who were taking their turn to clear up after a meal ditched the left-overs from everyone's plate into the mess gash tin which was then tipped over the ship's side. You'd often hear the familiar tinkling sound as a fork or spoon made its way down the steel gash chute into the ever-inviting oggin, often accompanied on its stately way by a rapturous cheer and round of applause from any matelots who happened to be nearby. If you were prone to discarding such items with the sort of careless abandon required then it could soon become very expensive for you.

It was during one of my initial clean-up sessions not long after I'd joined HMS *Loch Lomond* that I came across the rum container for the first time. This was a rather large and square aluminium bucket which, in naval parlance, was referred to as the Rum Fanny. It came with a big handle that was used for collecting the rum rations that were given to any man in the mess who was over 20 years old. This was issued on a daily basis as 'grog', made up of one part rum and three parts water. The Rum Fanny was, I have to say, a bit decrepit when I found it, so much so that I wondered how on earth it had been allowed to get into such a terrible state. I decided, there and then, to try and chip off the barnacles that were growing around the *inside* of the bucket, layer upon layer and with varying colour configurations. It really was the most disgusting sight and smelt absolutely rank. How could the liquid be dished out from such a filthy container day in and day out? This was the high point of most matelots' days and something everyone looked forward to.

Rum in the Navy was often used as a currency. A sippers here, a gulpers there. It worked wonders in keeping up the morale of a ship's company. When a man reached his 20th birthday, he was entitled to draw his first tot, enjoying, in the process, a sip from everyone else in the mess until, by the end of the day, he would be a complete write-off, good for nothing at all.

The issuing of that daily tot of rum was a naval tradition that ended in 1970 after concerns were raised that regular intakes of alcohol could lead to unsteady hands in those whose responsibility was working machinery. Was doing this a good thing? In my mind, yes it was. The safe and reliable operation of any piece of sophisticated machinery on the modern warship requires a specialist's complete and unfettered attention at all times. Beer, on the other hand, had been issued for some years before the tot stopped and continued afterwards, with the normal allowance of two cans a day.

This was, as you can imagine, subject to all sorts of abuse and, like the tot, ended up being used as an item of currency alongside the duty-free cigarette allowance of 300 cigarettes per month. I didn't smoke and either gave my coupons away or traded them for rum.

I had many attempts at chipping off the barnacles from the interior of the Rum Fanny although, as hard as I tried, I simply could not get it up to the standards that would be required at inspection. I then had no alternative but to report the state it was in to the mess killick whose exact words when he cast his eyes upon it cannot be recalled at this time – and if they could, they should never be put down on paper for anyone to read. In translation, I was at once informed that I was a stupid, fatherless, senseless idiot. I now knew, in no uncertain terms, just how sacrosanct the Rum Fanny was aboard any ship. This fact was emphasised to me by the killick's actions which resulted in my flying across the mess and ending up in the hammock netting. Further expletives were then offered, which I could only faintly hear in the background as there seemed to be a loud buzzing in my right ear where the killick had thumped me. Thus, after being thumped for doing what I thought was right, I learnt the valuable lesson that, no matter what sort of state it is in, one does not clean out a Rum Fanny. Ever.

In some ways, however, I was able to get my own back on that bullying killick. I was doing my usual work in the mess whilst the ship was taking on oil fuel from the Royal Fleet Auxiliary Tanker *Green Ranger* off the coast of Villa France in the Mediterranean. The forecast was poor but, as fuel was running dangerously low, the captain had little option but to try. Both ships were therefore steaming abreast into heavy seas and we had been warned to tie everything down. I therefore rather had my work cut out, lashing down crockery and anything that moved, when an almighty crunching sound drew my attention to the starboard side of the mess where the bows of the *Green Ranger* were now part of the room, having come through the side of the deck before, noisily, attempting to unravel itself from our mess and proceed.

Once it had done this, the large cavity that was left in our mess wall was, inevitably, besieged by the salt water of the Mediterranean, which came flooding in. I now had to very swiftly follow the damage control

instructions that had been taught to me in my initial training, my immediate reaction being to grab a couple of the nearest hammocks in order
to stuff them through the hole that had just been gouged into our ship's
side. Unfortunately, or fortunately for the others, one of the hammocks
I used, belonged to the killick of the mess. He'd always insisted that
his hammock was at the front of the hammock netting so he had swift
and easy access and, not long before the event I have described above,
I'd conceded defeat and succumbed to his wishes. That had meant, of
course, that I also had swift and easy access to his hammock and it was
the first to be used as part of the temporary patch I was now making up.

***

There was never a chance of falling into a dull routine in the Royal
Navy as someone, somewhere, was always dreaming up something new
for us to do. Thus it should have come as a surprise to no one when,
in 1951, the commander-in-chief Mediterranean came up with one of
his 'let's get the fleet out to sea' moments and decided to send my ship,
still then HMS *Loch Lomond*, as far away as possible from the boring and
unhealthy delights of Sliema Creek in Malta in order to steam 500 miles
east to Port Said, the entrance to the Suez Canal.

From there, we would transit this 100-mile-long desert shipping
canal through to the Red Sea port of Port Suez, continuing south for
another 150 miles or so, veering to port en route to pass what is now
Sharm-El-Sheikh, then sail another 100 miles up the Gulf of Aqaba,
the longest 'arm' of the Red Sea, in order to reside at Aqaba for nine
weeks or so. It was too deep to anchor at Aqaba which meant that the
engine room staff would be required to 'keep up steam' for that whole
nine-week period. 'We would be better off at sea' was one retort aimed
at the deaf ears of those who must be obeyed.

Aqaba's main claim to fame is that it hosted the exploits of Lieutenant
Colonel T.E. Lawrence, also known as Lawrence of Arabia. It lies at
the crossroads of four countries, namely Egypt, Palestine, Saudi Arabia
and Jordan. Aqaba is Jordan's only outlet to the sea for a country that

is otherwise landlocked. It all sounds very glamorous, an exotic setting full of potential and mystery – but the only thing we had to occupy our time when we were there was the occasional 'banyan', in other words, a beach party where we could amuse ourselves with beer and sandwiches. We had anticipated some excitement, as we would be permitted to fire upon aircraft of a certain nation if they ever came into range. None were ever seen.

As for getting mail whilst we were out there, something which might provide the occasional bright spot in day after day of monotony, that was very much a hit-or-miss affair. The mail was dropped in supposedly 'secure containers' by the RAF from their base at Fayid in Egypt. More often than not, these containers would burst open as they hit the water, scattering letters and parcels everywhere. These floated for only a short period of time before being engulfed and quickly sinking into the murky depths, followed soon afterwards by the damaged container which, on occasion, would sink as soon as it hit the water, thus taking all of its precious contents with it to that watery grave.

Every two weeks or so, a freshwater carrier would arrive from Port Suez, chugging sedately up the gulf at about eight knots. This very welcome visitor would also carry urgent spares, medical supplies and cartons of beer to be sold in the NAAFI shop on board. We couldn't get too carried away with such luxuries, however, since, our beer ration was still limited to two cans a day. Another way of cooling down was to take to the clear waters of the gulf ourselves, although it was a little dodgy. Local legend had it that 'George', supposedly a huge man-eating shark (a creature that, I hasten to add, was never seen or even picked up by the ship's sonar) was forever patrolling the local waters. As a consequence of this, lookouts were always posted on the ship's deck when people were swimming, armed with automatic weapons just in case 'George' made an unexpected appearance.

Soon after arriving at this extremely hot hell-hole, the ship's company became very friendly with the Palestine police force who kindly agreed to let us use their football pitch. I say 'pitch' but that doesn't mean it was anything like the sort of football pitch you or I would be familiar with, particularly today. For one thing, it didn't have a single blade of grass on it, and the packed and very dry earth that it was marked out on was as hard and unforgiving as concrete. We were all, regardless of that, very happy to have the opportunity to play a little football but it wasn't so very long before the ship's sick bay ran out of bandages and plasters. Our regular opponents, the aforementioned policemen, were all avid smokers so very much appreciated the occasional packet of 20 Royal Navy 'Blue Liner' cigarettes that would occasionally pass between us. Maybe that is why they were so keen to let us use their pitch.

Whilst we were out in the gulf, we received an invitation to trek northwards and into the scorching Jordanian desert towards the ancient city of Petra which, remarkably, only a few on board the ship had even heard of. Petra, for those of you who are still unfamiliar with the name, is a site that has been inhabited since prehistoric times, an important crossroads throughout history between Arabia, Egypt and Syria-Phoenicia. Petra is half-built and half-carved into the surrounding rock faces and is itself surrounded by numerous mountains, all of which are riddled with winding passages and deep gorges.

It is one of the world's most famous archaeological sites, one which I felt privileged to have the opportunity to visit. The trip was scheduled to last for six days which meant changing some duty rosters around on board so that the twelve of us who had been invited to go could be spared their watch responsibilities. Fortunately, I was one of the few who were selected to go and went without that much accompanying information – or even easy access to it from the locals as there were language difficulties to overcome.

The first part of our journey was made in an open-backed canvas-covered lorry. This seemed to go on for ages with our driver able, apparently, to seek out and drive over every single pothole possible on what passed for a road before we came, eventually, to an oasis that housed, complete with mules, a police patrol. Despite being in the desert, our attempts to settle down and try to get some sleep were marred by the bitter cold of the desert night; the light clothes we were all wearing provided us with no warmth whatsoever. No one had told us that, in the aptly named Valley of the Moon, the days would be scorching hot but the nights freezing cold. It was good, therefore, to eventually stir after a poor night's sleep to the braying of the mules and, wonderfully, the aroma of a hearty breakfast that included fried eggs and bacon as well as English tea that was rustled up for us by those policemen. The mules were to be our next mode of transport and as we prepared ourselves for the off, I couldn't help but notice, and not for the first time, that the blessed sand all around us got everywhere – and I mean *everywhere*.

One by one we were assisted as we mounted our mules, the doughty beasts that would take us to our final destination, the mysterious city of Petra, the 'sandstone city'. My mule behaved itself quite well but one or two of my fellow travellers did go on to find out how well gravity can be demonstrated if you are sat on the back of a reluctant mule. Fortunately, although the journey was suitably chaotic throughout, there were no broken bones to report, despite each of the mules being quite determined to find their own direction and speed of advance throughout.

After a while of having nothing to gaze upon but rocks and sand, some green vegetation, sparse at first, began to dot the land around us, eventually becoming so dense that our mules decided, as one, that they didn't want to proceed any further. You cannot, as I found out, force or cajole a mule to do something that it doesn't want to do: once it has decided that it has had enough of something, that is that. So we dismounted from our four-legged companions and prepared to complete the journey on the two legs that we could call our own, although the immediate priority was to rid ourselves of the ever-present sand and make our now very sore backsides as comfortable as possible.

We eventually became aware of a huge rampart of sandstone rearing up ahead of us from the thick and overgrown green vegetation. The policemen who had accompanied us throughout had a rough idea of where we were, but even they had some difficulty in finding the entrance to this enormous city that had first been carved out of the sandstone around one and a half thousand years earlier. Each of us was given a machete before forming into two groups which were tasked with cutting down the undergrowth in order to find out where the entrance to Petra was. And, after several attempts over different routes, an entrance was eventually found, one that had remained cleverly concealed right to the very end. Thus, meandering in single file in a manner which very much made me think of the old saying about the blind leading the blind, we squeezed, one by one, through a very narrow gap in the huge rock face until, almost without warning, we stumbled upon a much larger opening which displayed – radiated even – a sight none of us could ever have seen or visualised before. I found my first sight of the ancient city of Petra to be absolutely staggering. As I gazed up at its beautifully carved sandstone buildings, the majority of which had been hewn out of the sheer rock at such a great height, I wondered how on earth this unusual and visually spectacular splendour could possibly have been achieved.

Littered everywhere were pieces of broken crockery amongst many more unbroken damaged pots and other vessels of all sizes and shapes. We were warned to be careful where we trod and on no account to remove any of the thousands of artefacts that we were now surrounded by, even the smallest of the broken pieces – damaged, we were told, by the comings and goings of animals over the passage of time. I was completely taken aback by it all, the scale and majesty of the construction and the amazing workmanship that would have been needed to produce all of the different buildings, some of which seemed to be hanging in space around two hundred feet from the floor. The attention to detail was absolutely staggering. It was, and remains, a sight that I have never forgotten. Eventually, however, we had to make our reluctant way back to the oasis where we had spent the previous night, able, at last, to take a nice cool bath and to scrape out, in the process, all of the sand that had found its way into hitherto invisible and unknown bodily crevices.

I must, at this point, quickly deviate from the narrative and tell you about another memorable visit we made at around that time. This was to Olympia in Greece (in 1952) where I was fortunate enough to attend the lighting of the flame for that year's Olympic Games which were to be held at Helsinki in Finland. Because Olympia is the site where the Olympic Games were first held, the torch is lit there and makes its way to the host city, never being extinguished en route, before, finally, being used to light the beacon that burns its way throughout the time the games are held – in this case, in Helsinki's Olympic Stadium. For such a time-honoured and ancient ceremony mind you, the weather on the day was utterly dreadful as it was very wet and hardly stopped raining for the duration of the ceremony.

This was particularly unfortunate for the several celestial virgins who were, as tradition demanded, in attendance, all clad in white outfits that got absolutely soaked and clung to their skin. Given the conditions on the day, quite how the Olympic torch was lit and then stayed that way is a mystery but, somehow, the officials got a healthy flame and it was on its way. I took a photograph of that moment but it ended up looking as dreary as the weather which, although windy and wet, was at least mild enough to keep the celestial virgins warm! We'd had an interesting journey getting there, sailing through the Corinth Canal en route and having to hang fenders (a 'bumper' used to absorb the kinetic energy of a boat or vessel berthing against a jetty, quay wall, another vessel – or, as in this case, the sheer rock sides of the canal) over the ship's side just in case things didn't go quite to plan, as it was possible, in places, to touch the sides during this four-mile-long short cut from the Gulf of Corinth to the Aegean Sea.

Lighting the Olympic Flag at Olympia in 1952 (courtesy Tony Beasley)

***

It was not only excursions such as this that disrupted the normal routine of shipboard life. Whilst I was out in the Mediterranean with HMS *Loch Lomond*, the ship was sent to one of Malta's dry docks to have its bottom scraped as well as having some general maintenance work carried out. With little to no need of me or my duties aboard at this time, I was therefore ordered to report to HMS *Magpie* to carry out whatever duties were deemed suitable whilst they had me. This meant serving under HRH Prince Philip, commander of HMS *Magpie* from 1950 to 1952. It was, despite HRH being in charge, the junior ship in our squadron and was therefore known, with affection, as the 'canteen boat', in keeping with naval tradition. The two ships and ships' companies were fairly familiar to one another anyway. Prince Philip would generally berth *Magpie* to anything that was available that would conveniently facilitate all of his comings and goings, with *Loch Lomond* often tying up alongside if double berthing allowed it, meaning that, even when I was seconded to *Magpie*, my first ship was never far away. Everyone seemed to know Prince Philip and it didn't matter if you were on a lonely Greek island or some pokey little place in the middle of the Aegean, there'd always be someone there who knew him.

During my time on HMS *Magpie* 'with' HRH Prince Philip, we always seemed to visit the 'better' places in the Mediterranean: Cannes, Port Said and Alexandria, for example, although the latter two places were still adjusting to life after the war. Cannes was lovely, but a week's pay barely paid for a cup of coffee there!

The original signal that had come through to HMS *Loch Lomond* had outlined that the reason for my short stay on HRH's ship would be 'for experience'. The experience in question consisted of reading countless reams of Morse-coded signals, five-letter groups, often four or five hundred at a time – and doing it all with an old-fashioned (now) typewriter. It wasn't that onerous a task for me as we had been taught to touch-type during my initial training at HMS *Ganges* in Ipswich. What I wasn't quite so prepared for was the sheer number of coded messages that were sent to *Magpie*: there were hundreds and hundreds of them.

More often than not, I'd be sat receiving them in rough weather, usually storms of force nine and ten. The Mediterranean doesn't have any tides but, believe me, it can get rough!

That period spent on loan to HMS *Magpie* proved beneficial in one very significant way to me as my service documents for that time showed that I was 'Proficient in reading Morse with a typewriter'. This was just as well really because Morse code was then the only means of communicating with both ship and shore whilst at sea. It was normally sent by tape at around 25 words a minute or, when traffic was building up, a higher rate than that. These higher speeds ended up defeating the object as faster Morse resulted in more repeats being requested by the people receiving them which meant, of course, that the broadcast frequencies ended up being even more cluttered than they had been. Morse was broadcast in the four, eight, twelve and sixteen megacycle wavelengths. And, just like you trying to tune into your favourite radio station on one of the older type radios, reception, depending on where you were in the world, varied considerably in terms of quality. It was often the case, for example, that when a ship was in the Indian Ocean, then the best readable reception came from a broadcast station in Halifax, Nova Scotia; or when you were sailing in the Mediterranean, then the best signal came from Portishead radio in the UK. The main broadcast stations were Lascaris wireless in Malta, Kranji wireless in Singapore, Hong Kong wireless, Colombo wireless in Ceylon (now Sri Lanka), Halifax wireless in Nova Scotia (Canada) and Admiralty wireless back in the UK.

Each of these shore radio stations also served ships at sea with ship-to-shore High Frequency (HF) systems that mainly operated in the frequency ranges of the broadcast. These principal radio stations were also connected to each other by a landline which meant that the Admiralty in London could, in theory, establish communication links with any of its warships, no matter where they were in the world. But, as I've said: that was in theory! The Admiralty also used a Very Low Frequency (VLF) broadcast for submarines. This was transmitted from Rugby (a small English town) and had the call sign GBR. These operated on 16 kilocycles and could be read in most parts of the world by any of the Royal Navy's submarines, providing they were submerged at a depth of 33 feet or more. As a comparison, the Russian Northern Fleet operated their broadcast from an area in the North-East Ural mountains, their call sign was UBS and they transmitted on 23 kilocycles. Needless to say, we'd be listening out for each other just as we did for our own broadcast traffic which I had to 'crack', regardless of whether the information concerned us or not. This would be done on a Typex coding machine which wasn't all that different to the wartime Enigma machines. These coded messages could be, more often than not, up to a thousand words long. But it didn't faze me. I seemed to have a natural talent with codes and ciphers and, later on in my naval career, would spend many hours working with codes used by the old Soviet Union, China and numerous other countries.

My short period serving aboard HMS *Magpie* came to an abrupt end when both of 'my' ships, *Loch Lomond* and *Magpie*, ended up playing each other in the final of the squadrons' football match at St Angelo. With Malta having a reliably hot and dry climate, the football pitches out there, especially in St Angelo, were extremely formidable. They'd either been brushed or blown dry by the prevailing winds and were rock hard, dusty, full of pot holes and dangerously unattractive to look at, let alone play on. They were so bad that I reckon the War Pensions Agency

HMS *Magpie* (courtesy www.naval-history.net)

must, even today, still be paying out thousands of pounds to assorted ex-servicemen as compensation for the injuries they sustained playing on those grassless and extremely hard pitches. Fortunately, on this occasion, that wasn't a problem that I had to worry about as I'd secured myself the task of commentating. I ended up standing behind *Magpie*'s goal with a group of my messmates from *Loch Lomond*. I was, I have to say, being rather over-enthusiastic in my commentary efforts and was rather biased towards my own ship – so much so that my regular biting and sarcastic comments about *Magpie*'s team encouraged a tidal wave of retorts and wardroom clichés that were, for me, the sort that had hitherto been unheard of, such was the imagination being used in creating them. This continued and I soon gathered that my birthright was now being brought into question by anyone and everyone connected with HMS *Magpie*.

That evening I was made aware of a draft chit sent by the coxswain from HMS *Loch Lomond* that requested my immediate return back to that ship. No mention of the football commentary 'incident' had been made, at least officially, but, bearing in mind the abuse I'd been receiving, there was one casualty, that being my underpants and the nasty brown stain that had suddenly appeared there. That chit and my imminent return to *Loch Lomond* were serious enough, however, for me to realise that reprisals in the form of my spending time at His Majesty's Pleasure via incarceration in the hell-hole of one of Malta's detention centres was a very real possibility. Inevitably, I hadn't been back on HMS *Loch Lomond* for long before comments about my sudden departure from the commentary scene were being made – although, as I happily noticed, the squadron trophy, awarded to the victorious team, was fully visible on the QM's desk at the top of the gangway with, marked on a blackboard next to it, the words '*Magpie Thrashed – Royal prerogative and all that 2-0*'.

The QM didn't get away with such partisanship either and was awarded three days' stoppage of leave for that bit of apparently treasonable script! Yet, as we sailed at noon, it no longer mattered, and by tot time, lots of inevitable cartoons about the previous day's events were appearing on the ship's main notice board. Some of the accompanying quips were royally hilarious and worthy of much journalistic praise. As for me, the worst of it was the fact that I ended up with a thick head and a taste in my mouth that couldn't have been too dissimilar from the sort you'd get from sampling a Japanese wrestler's jockstrap. But then I had been offered (and was too proud to turn down) many a sipper of rum for the amusement that my abortive (but fun while it lasted) commentary on that memorable football match had caused.

I went on to serve for a happy, if fairly uneventful twelve months on HMS *Loch Lomond* before I was advanced up the ranks to an ordinary telegraphist and transferred to HMS *Fierce*, an Algerine (class originally built for the Royal Navy and Royal Canadian Navy during the war) that was also the squadron leader of three other similar ships of that class. Life on board HMS *Fierce* saw us spend most of our time sweeping mines off the Corfu channel[1] in a minefield that has been designated QBY 827. There's no variety in minesweeping. It is what the ship was built for and it is what you are trained to do. Every day. Sweeping consequently started at sun-up and continued all the way through to sunset. QBY 827 was the area of the Corfu channel between Corfu itself and the Albanian coastline, one that British minesweepers had already been working in almost immediately after hostilities with Nazi Germany had ended, operations that they had previously thought had been successful. But this was not the case.

Back in 1946, part of the immediate post-war Mediterranean fleet had assembled off the Greek coast at Argostoli for the fleet regatta. This group comprised HMS *Saumarez*, a destroyer and fleet leader, and HMS *Volage*, another destroyer, one that had seen action in both the Arctic and Indian Oceans during the war. They were joined by two other ships, thus making up a small fleet, all steaming in line with HMS *Saumarez* the second ship in the line. Sadly, for ship and crew, that made them vulnerable to anything that might have been displaced or washed astern from the leading ship and that is exactly what happened. A mine that was disturbed by the wash ended up being sucked in and under HMS *Saumarez*, hitting it and exploding under the bridge.

---

1 A narrow body of water along the coasts of Albania and Greece to the east, that separates those two countries from the Greek island of Corfu on the west.

The resulting blast killed 36 of the ship's company and injured many others.

HMS *Volage* was immediately ordered to take *Saumarez* in tow. On doing so, *Volage* hit another mine; the blast from that blew its bows off and killed eight of the ship's company, most of whom were in the forward mess. Many others were injured. The HM Hospital Ship *Maine* was, fortunately, in the area and able to swiftly attend and treat the injured; the dead were buried in Corfu cemetery with full Royal Naval honours. This tragic event was seared into the minds of everyone in similar positions on Royal Navy ships and we all took the task of minesweeping very seriously and with the professionalism and attention to detail that you would expect.

HMS *Fierce* was one of the minesweepers that was redeployed back to that area of ocean with orders to recommence sweeping for mines, our dawn-till-dusk role. Further mines were indeed swept and found to have been of German origin and, almost certainly, laid after hostilities had ended and *after* the initial period of minesweeping had been completed. As to whoever the culprits were who re-laid the mines, that was never discovered and no one has ever owned up to doing it, although I have long had my suspicions and will return to this point shortly.

As a telegraphist, I often found myself off the ship and on a nearby beach during minesweeping operations, giving directions as to when the sweepers should turn. It was a case, for them, of going up and down a stretch of water, time and time again, day after day after day, up and down repeatedly. It was a very tedious task and became, for me, so boring in its execution, that I now look back at that time and wonder why the daily blaze of a hot sun on me as I paced those white, sandy and deserted sandy beaches didn't drive me mad. Minesweeping sounds exciting but I never once saw a mine explode. We successfully swept dozens, bringing them to the surface only to sink them again, courtesy of small arms fire from a .303 gun. The mines in question were the traditional horned type that you might see in wartime films. They had a detonator in the tip of each of these horns so the mine would explode if any of these was hit. But our task was to sink them rather than blow them up and we did that to hundreds of mines, all of which will now have settled into the sediment and sand that surrounds Corfu.

My job as a telegraphist, which involved using a typewriter to receive taped Morse at 25 words per minute, was fairly easy – that is, until you combined it with the problems that were inevitably encountered if you are steering with the swell. In those circumstances, the typewriter carriage return decides to adopt a mind of its own. To top all of that off, we would also have to contend with absolutely atrocious radio reception which was, at the time, a permanent problem in the Mediterranean unless, it seemed, you wanted to read signals from Singapore or Halifax. Take Malta as an example. I might well have been within visual distance of the island yet, if we needed signal traffic to get there we'd have to send that signal via Hong Kong, Singapore, Halifax or even Portishead radio, the inevitability of that being that an extra load was being put onto the landlines of Malta.

There were breaks in the monotony, mind you. Around every six weeks, the squadron would shift from its position off the sandy shores of Greece and sail over to Famagusta in Cyprus where we'd stay put for around ten days in order to take on ship's mail as well as fresh water, greens, real milk and the inevitable oranges which were available for us to buy for just one penny for a baker's dozen. Other ports we'd call in at this time were Split on Yugoslavia's Dalmatian coast, Iskenderun in Turkey or Piraeus in Greece. You might think that such exotic ports would have no end of temptations available for a young sailor but, as I was still under twenty at the time, my shore time expired at 2100 so the combination of that, plus the fact my weekly pay was just £1.12s.6d a week, meant that, for me, the pleasures of life on offer in those places were not going to be experienced very often, if at all!

I was lucky really. The queues outside sickbay after such runs ashore would normally be quite long and 'Rose Cottage' as it is referred to in the Royal Navy (a clinic for treating exotic 'social' diseases) would be rather full with one poor consolation being that you got your own knife, fork, spoon, cup and plate for the duration of your stay. Thus, as you'd expect, the locals would always enjoy our visits, especially those in Famagusta. We sailed from there for the last time in 1953 to a spectacular send-off – talk about the people crying in the streets! We were pelted with oranges until the range was too great so there were plenty of those to go around. It was a place that we all loved as well as the wonderful people who lived there. It was only a small fishing village (although it did possess the deepest harbour on Cyprus) but it was full of character, a wonderful place to go after minesweeping for anything up to six weeks at a time.

***

Every ship in the Navy carries its own contribution towards everyday life and making it appear as 'normal' as possible. Every mess deck, for example, has its own duty comedian and sky pilot (military chaplain) as well as a lower-deck lawyer; mess-deck tealeaf (thief); a crabby bastard; a snivelling or grovelling bastard; bullet maker; bullet firer; punchy; stores pilferer; phantom flipper; canteen ranger; sickbay ranger; ship's stallion and gopher. Some of those you can probably work out for yourselves, some might need explaining to you. But all of them have their place within the tight confines of a ship in which you could be encapsulated for two and half to three years, time that was often spent in states of utter boredom. Except for the moments when that boredom was relieved...

On one particular occasion, the men who had been on duty for the morning watch (0400–0800) were in the forward bathroom engaged in using up most of the day's ration of water trying to get a lather from the soap that they had acquired, by fair means or foul, from the buffers' (the senior sailors') store.

Amidst the early morning hubbub, one of the ship's cooks, a character by the name of Dodger Long, burst into the bathroom shouting at the top of his voice, 'There's a party [woman] in her knicks and bra in the forward cabin on *Magpie!*'

'Bullshit,' replied someone.

'Fly your kite!' cried another.

'It's true, it's bladdy true,' insisted Dodger, so excited now that he was swinging to and fro like the pendulum on a grandfather clock.

'I'll put a week's tot on it,' he added.

This confident statement triggered the inevitable mad dash towards the upper deck where, sure enough, there was a female presence just visible through the starboard scuttle, or porthole, on one of the Magpie's cabins. She was wearing light blue underwear and was visible from her shoulders to her knees. As you can imagine, the buzz that this stirred went around the ship like greased lightning and before long, some twenty hairy-arsed sailors, some with towels draped around their waists, were all in attendance, boggle-eyed at the sight before them as, one by one, they caught a glimpse of the scantily clad female in question.

The excitement around the ship continued to rise and it wasn't long before the guardrail on our port side was buckling under the sheer weight of a couple of dozen sex-starved sailors. Sadly, our reverie was soon to be shattered by a strident voice emanating from the bridge of *Magpie*. It was the officer of the watch whose loud but unintelligible exclamations and movements (his arms were gesticulating like those of a monkey caught by his balls in a rat trap) were unavoidable. We had to assume, by the noise he was making together with those exaggerated body movements, that he wanted us all to move on.

That assumption was correct as the buzz that was still going around the mess deck was interrupted by hearing the following instruction via our quartermaster's pipe.

'Do you hear there, all hands muster on the starboard side of the upper deck and at the double. Stand fast all those actually on watch.'

Upon hearing this, the gathered matelots were, not unnaturally, somewhat unimpressed. It was, after all, a long time since any of them had seen an attractive young female, excepting, that is, those who could be seen on the deck of a Royal Fleet Auxiliary replenishment ship. So it was, by and large, a comfort that was accessible only to the privileged few. However, a piped order is an order, so, reluctantly, everyone assembled as requested and listened in as Jimmy, our beloved first lieutenant, outlined the reasoning behind this somewhat out-of-the-blue mustering of the ship's crew.

'Some of you shower, particularly those who stood on the morning watch, have caused uproar between the captain and *Magpie*'s company.

The guilty ones will know exactly what I mean so, to save further embarrassment, I want the men responsible to come forward and NOW!'

Not a man moved. Deadly hush. One could clearly hear the choppy waters sloshing between the two ships and the shrieks of two shitehawks[2] that were circling above our gathered heads, the small white deposits that they were regularly emitting intended, we hoped, for the first lieutenant.

'What the bloody hell is he going on about?' mumbled Chalky White, ship's duty comedian.

'White, here!' bawled the coxswain in response. He was a short and very dapper chief petty officer, a vintage who had served in the First World War and who was normally quite tolerant before tot time. He didn't look too tolerant as he quizzed Chalky.

'What did you say?'

'Nothing 'swain.'

'NOTHING? I distinctly heard you say something, White.'

'All I said Chief, er, sorry, 'swain, was I bet some bastard swipes my dinky spud peeling knife whilst I'm standing here like a spare prick at a wedding.'

'For your information, White, the whole ship's company are mustered and no one, but no one, would want to touch your bloody spud peeler.'

'It's not bloody, 'swain...'

'It soon will be. Now, was it you on the upper deck who saw what you saw?'

'Saw what I saw what, 'swain?'

Give Chalky his due, he wasn't letting the coxswain have his way.

'You know bloody well what I'm on about. Get down to my office, I'll sort you out later.'

Sensing he needed to take part in the proceedings again, the first lieutenant now stepped back into the fray and spoke again. He was probably wondering quite what all the fuss was about, having only just been turned out of his pit.

---

2 Seagulls.

'Now the rest of you listen. I want every man jack who knows what was so interesting on the port side of the upper deck just now to come forward.'

The stand-off continued. Not a soul moved. Chalky White had gone below to see what the coxswain had to say to him in the confines of his office; it certainly looked as if he, at least, was for the high jump. Most of those assembled hadn't the faintest idea what the cox had been ranting and raving about. You could, perhaps, understand such a rattled demeanour if it had been after tot time, when he was known to be 'difficult' after sinking too many pink gins at a penny a shot, but never at 0930 in the forenoon – except, that is, after a famous binge in the wardroom one night. That particular incident had seen all of the wardroom end up walking around in a half-pissed state with the sole exception of the navigating officer, a young sub-lieutenant who was recently out of Dartmouth ('Daddy is an admiral you know') who wouldn't say boo to an albatross.

I'm digressing. Back to the incident on the two ships.

The first lieutenant now started on us again. 'You'll bloody well stay mustered and at attention until I get those responsible to own up,' he bellowed, adding, 'I am reliably informed that about a dozen or more of you rabble know exactly what I'm on about, so come on, let's have you or you'll stay here till you drop.'

Picture the scene. It was just after 0930, the sun was belting down straight through the deck awning and flies were mingling amidst the pong of the gash (rubbish) boat which was alongside us, that particular smell now mingling with the carbon monoxide fumes that were coming from the forward boiler. So, not unnaturally, after around twenty minutes or so, the lines of bewildered sailors began to sway and fidget, almost in unison.

'Stand still, Blenkinsopp.'

'I feel faint 'swain.'

'You'll feel more than bloody faint unless those responsible step forward. They know who I mean.'

Blenkinsopp was one of the telegraphists who, at a height of six feet, eight inches, was usually referred to as 'Lofty', or, by us specialists in the communications mess, as 'the whip aerial' as, despite his height, he weighed about nine stone and had difficulty in standing at the best of times.

Now Jumper Collins, who also had difficulty in standing even under normal conditions, due to his tiny feet, stepped forward, immediately followed by the Doc with Jumper's oppo, Sharky Ward, hard on his heels. Then, before the coxswain could utter another word, the delight on Jimmy's face fell into his lower jaw as the whole of the cooks, stewards, communications and seaman's departments stepped forward in one smart moment that was so slick it wouldn't even have been equalled by a squad of Royal Marines from outside Buckingham Palace.

Not a word was spoken. For once, Jimmy was gobsmacked. He stared at the coxswain and shouted, 'Do something, coxswain. What are you bloody well on board for?'

'Ballast,' muttered one of the chefs in a voice designed to be heard.

'I 'eard that Jones, I'll deal with you later.'

Our captain, having finished a conflab with *Magpie's* first lieutenant, now re-emerged from behind a turret and started to discuss the situation with his, that is to say, our first lieutenant. And he was, let's make no mistake about it, absolutely seething, with one of the anguished phrases he was heard to say being something along the lines of '…our good relations with Prince Philip'.

After the captain had taken his leave of our group, the first lieutenant stated, in a confident and calm manner, that the ship would be getting under way in half an hour, so hands to muster for leaving harbour and ship's company… dismiss!

'I thought we'd be here for two days,' dripped Shiner Wright, the ship's lower-deck lawyer in a voice that, inevitably, carried to the coxswain.

'Well you are bloody well wrong… again, Wright – so get moving.'

I wondered how Taffy Jones was going to be 'dealt with'. A three-badge-dipped chief, he had hooked up with the coxswain sometime before the year dot and the two of them were as thick as thieves. They were once shore-going oppos until, one night, a fight developed at Aggie's in Portsmouth concerning the affections of a 'lady of the night'. The naval police (crushers) were soon on the scene, and grabbing Taffy by the proverbials they unceremoniously slung him into the back of a meat wagon for his trip to the cooler where he would now be spending the night. The following morning, however, the coxswain wanted all charges levelled against Taffy dropped, despite the fact that the 'crushers' had already submitted their patrol report. However, Taffy ended up facing a commodore's punishment.

When he got to the commodore's table after the best part of a fortnight locked up with no contact with the outside world and only a Bible to read, Taffy Jones was not in the best of moods.

It didn't help that the master-at-arms who'd be deciding Taff's fate was a born bastard, as thick as six foot of road and a certified groveller.

'Now then Jones, do you have anything to say?'

Silence.

'Jones, the commodore asked if you had anything to say?'

'I'm not fucking deaf,' shouted Taff.

'We do not have that sort of language here, Jones,' interjected the po-faced commodore. He now turned to Taffy's divisional officer, a sub-lieutenant who was all of twenty years old and still suffering from the nappy rash he'd sustained whilst training at Dartmouth.

'Now then, sub, what can you tell us about Chief Petty Officer Jones?'

Saluting in the manner of a guardsman and snapping his heels together as swiftly and sharply as a shark closing its jaws, the sub-lieutenant began to outline Taffy's history.

'He has been on board for some time sir, two commissions in fact. I would say about three years, sir.'

Taffy was now fuming. 'Sir this, sir that. You haven't a bloody clue who I am, have you? Call yourself my divisional officer? I've got four kids older than you.'

'Shut *up* Jones,' bellowed the master-at-arms.

'No I fucking won't. He has never spoken to me in all the five weeks he's been aboard. I run the whole department and he fucking well knows it. How on earth can a young sprog like him give a character reference to a chief petty officer who has been in the Andrew [Royal Navy] for longer than he has been on this fucking earth?'

The commodore's response to this outburst was one of sheer amazement. Senior ratings did not normally react like this and he may secretly have been impressed to hear Taffy talk as he did, even though, 'officially', it wasn't the done thing.

'Now Jones, calm down. I can understand your frustration but you are here before me on a very serious charge and in order to get a picture of how you perform on board, I have to ask your divisional officer certain questions.'

'I know that sir, but how can a sub-lieutenant, still wearing Dartmouth dampers, tell you about me when he has hardly set eyes on me, never mind actually speak to me. It's bloody ridiculous.'

Despite the kernel of truth in what Taffy was saying and the inclination of the commodore to believe what he was saying, he still had to be seen to be dealt with for his outburst and misconduct. That meant he was reduced to the ranks and, in addition to that, was deprived of all three of his good conduct badges.

His divisional officer, on the other hand, was sent ashore to be 're-educated'.

***

During the course of our minesweeping duties, HMS *Fierce* was summoned to a Maltese dockyard for an extensive refit. One of the duties involved assorted members of *Fierce's* ship's company being mustered into 'chipping parties', meaning that they were all slung into cradles and dangled over the ship's side so that they could chip off all the old paint from the sides ready for the application of a shellac-based primer before repainting it. One of our number, a particularly enthusiastic (yes, I really was!) leading telegraphist, was busily chipping away on the starboard bow and, in the process, managed to put a hole through one of the plates. This merited further investigation, the result of which found that HMS *Fierce* was unseaworthy. This led to all of the ship's company being immediately transferred to HMS *Recruit*, another minesweeper and one which had been part of the massive invasion force from Portsmouth on D-Day, now brought out of mothballs to cover for our temporarily incapacitated ship.

Interestingly, my service documents, which both the MOD and Norcross (the MOD's Veterans UK association, which is based in Thornton-Cleveleys) treat as absolutely sacrosanct, do not show this particular ship change on my service records. HMS *Recruit*, however, previously mothballed, is shown on the list of ships that took part in the 1953 fleet review. It would seem, therefore that, as far as the MOD were concerned, although we were now serving on a different ship it was, to all intents and purposes, still HMS *Fierce*.

After spending two and a half years in Mediterranean waters, our squadron of four minesweepers began to sail for home, with each minesweeper having an added responsibility of towing two motor launches (MLs). However, nature being what it is, the MLs failed to stay attached to their respective ships and, one by one, parted company with us in the Bay of Biscay. That isn't particularly surprising as it is hardly the most tranquil area of open water in the world. I vaguely remember that the senior officer of our little fleet was becoming just a little bit agitated at the thought of four MLs drifting helplessly in the seas of Biscay, becoming, as he so correctly said, a very real and present danger to the other ships that sailed in this area.

This was, naturally, all the action-starved gunners on the ships needed to prepare themselves for a little bit of unexpected action and, sure enough, it was announced that the eight drifting MLs were to be located and sunk by gunfire. But even this little practical diversion was not to be because, after a short time, it was announced that all eight MLs had been lost and could not even be traced on radar. Hardly surprising. The weather, even for the Bay of Biscay, was absolutely diabolical, blowing a force nine to ten with attendant heavy seas, so it was logical to assume that all of the MLs had capsized and found their way down to join Davy Jones in his locker.

A sobering thought for us all as we sailed closer and closer to home.

CHAPTER 4

Radio Warfare

'You could, I promise you, have heard a pin drop. We were all stunned, completely and utterly stunned.'

Having spent over two years at sea, I returned from foreign service in May 1953 in order to join the Royal Navy Signal School at HMS *Mercury*. This was an onshore facility based near Petersfield in Hampshire. It was known for having a 'small ship' rating – in other words, it was a crabby (unkempt or grubby) but happy place. It was an opportune posting for me at that time of my naval career, for it was now time for me to be well and truly initiated into the communications world. This would involve learning about and undergoing practical training in the use of new types of transmitters, receivers, codes, ciphers, aerials and all the other procedures we were now expected to be familiar with. Leydene House, which is where HMS *Mercury* was based, had been purchased by the Admiralty in 1941. It had previously been owned by Lord and Lady Peel; he was the grandson of Robert Peel, the founder of our modern-day police force. This large country house, now the rather grand and exclusive property of the Admiralty, was right in the middle of nowhere in rural Hampshire, about 20 miles north of Portsmouth and 888 feet above sea level, overlooking the lovely Meon Valley and picturesque village of East Meon. On a clear day, you could see the Isle of Wight from the top of the senior rates' mess.

I'm not joking when I say that this most important of naval bases was in the middle of nowhere. It was very isolated and quite often inaccessible.

Petersfield was the nearest railway station and that was eight miles away, whilst the roads to Leydene were sometimes closed because of severe local weather conditions. The winter of 1963 comes immediately to mind, because we were stuck there several days, cut off from the rest of the world by a blanket of snow. Why, then, if it was so isolated, had it been chosen as the new HQ of HMS *Mercury*? After all, its purpose was to teach the art of communication so there was a certain amount of irony in the fact that it was so remote and prone to being cut off, that there were times when communicating with the place itself became rather more difficult than anyone would care to admit.

The choice of Leydene for the Navy's new training school was made because of the frequent German raids on Portsmouth during the Second World War. Portsmouth dockyard, a key installation and obvious target for Luftwaffe bombers, housed what was then the Royal Navy Signal School. For both its own safety and protection and for the long-term security of the country, it had to be relocated. Doing so in a more remote and rural area didn't, of course, make HMS *Mercury* safe from any form of attack. But it did make the location a lot safer which, in turn, meant that it could focus on its job rather than having to worry about when the next raid might be. It wasn't the only Royal Navy base to be relocated away from Portsmouth either, for at around about the same time, the Admiralty were purchasing a country house at Southwick in order to relocate the Navy's Maritime Warfare School away from Portsmouth. It became HMS *Dryad* and was in use until 2004, when it was relocated again, this time to Fareham, where it is known as HMS *Collingwood*.

HMS *Mercury*'s comparatively remote location made it a very atmospheric place to live and work. It was often lost in fields of thick, low-lying cloud and, as I have already written, was also prone to being cut off from the rest of the world altogether. The nearest villages were Clanfield to the east, East Meon to the north and Hambledon, famous for being the 'home' of cricket, to the south. Fortunately for all of us, the villages all had decent public houses which were frequented by, and very popular with, the vast population of HMS *Mercury*. But, because it was situated on a hill, going ashore (you always 'go ashore' from a naval ship, even if it is a great house that stands 20 miles inland of the sea) for a pint was easy enough; the real challenge was, having had a few, getting back again along all the (uphill) twists and turns that now had to be negotiated en route. Buses were completely unheard of in that part of the world whilst official naval transport options were very few and far between, the rare chance of that being an option depending upon the sobriety of the officer of the watch (OOW).

Payday was every fortnight. If this much-anticipated day fell near a duty weekend, one of the duty watch would stay behind whilst everyone else would slip out under the cover of the surrounding woods (being in a remote location had its advantages) down to the Bat and Ball pub in Clanfield before hastily returning for fire drill at 1900. A new landlord had just, it was rumoured, been installed at the Bat and Ball; he was said to be a retired RAF squadron leader who didn't take too kindly to the senior service, who, he was alleged to have said, drove some of his 'better clientele' away. In reality of course, those communications matelots, myself included, were his bread and butter, especially in the winter when the only hint of cricket lay in his forever skew-whiff pictures and woodworm-laden cricketing artefacts, all of which seemed to be kept together by the blanket of cobwebs that adorned the scruffy walls of this otherwise old and very charming red-brick pub.

The OOW in my time was an experienced lower-rank communications officer who was responsible for the signal school at weekends. The majority of his duties were carried out for him by a quartermaster (QM), an experienced communications specialist who was himself assisted by the bosun's mate, a more junior member of the duty watch. One of the OOW's favourite pastimes was to dispatch a young sailor, armed with a twelve-inch wooden ruler, to trek all the way around the camp in order to measure the depth of water remaining in each of the seven huge static water tanks on site. This particular operation, a strenuous one at any time, was usually only instigated by this particularly sadistic OOW when the weather was blowing a hoolie with accompanying heavy rain or when the ground was under a foot or more of snow.

The OOW had a private room attached to the QM's office for the exclusive use of the OOW. This caboose was equipped with a telephone, bed, wash-basin, toilet, electric fire, curtains, carpets and, most importantly of all, the Rum Breaker, from which men arriving at Leydene from all corners of the globe were issued with their daily tot of rum. On one particular Sunday, Chalky White was the detailed duty bosun's mate in the QM's office. His responsibilities were to answer the telephone, take messages, wet the tea and generally assist the QM in whatever needed to be done. Whilst he was doing this, the other men of the duty watch were planning to 'nip out for a few pints' at the Bat and Ball in order to sound out the new landlord. Now, absconding from your place of designated duty required a sense of adventure and camaraderie, something which all young sailors have through sheer bloody necessity. Chalky had therefore been 'planted' with the QM and had been, in the process, fully briefed on what was required of him throughout the evening.

The well-worn route to the Bat and Ball was down the lower boardwalk and through to the woods before heading out onto the road that led to an overgrown and seldom-used rear entrance to the public bar. It came as a bit of a surprise, therefore, to the landlord when, on a busy and sunny Sunday lunchtime, a bunch of exuberant and thirsty matelots, all of whom were clad in their working gear, were seen clambering through his establishment's previously unsullied rear entrance. The landlord, faced with a quiet and profitless Sunday, had resorted, it seems, to making himself busy by propping himself up against his own bar, small tumbler of beer in one hand and a half-smoked cheroot in the other; so, for him, the sudden distraction offered by our motley incoming shower was a bit of a game changer.

As slovenly as they all were, he could now hear the sound of coins tinkling into an otherwise almost motionless till. Now, at the blink of an eye, his clientele had swelled and he sprang into action lest they change their mind and go elsewhere. It wasn't long after the first couple of pints had been swiftly imbibed that the inevitable Sunday sing-song broke out, much to the delight, it has to be said, of the handful of morbid-looking locals who, with some anticipation, had been looking forward to the usual sods' opera (songs sung by soldiers or sailors in order to entertain themselves) to break out, something they had all become accustomed to before old misery guts, as the new landlord was known, had taken over as landlord and threatened, amongst other things, to ban, along with those who dared to sing them.

Things were livening up.

Following the sinking of the second pint, Dodger Long was unanimously nominated to order the third. He duly went to the bar where, as he stood there waiting to be served, he overheard the landlord blistering away to someone on the telephone. Dodger was able to pick up some of what he was saying and worked out that the landlord was deep in conversation with our plant in the OOW's office, one Chalky White. The words 'duty watch', 'trouble' and 'noise' were picked out and, from that, Dodger had little doubt in what direction the dialogue was heading, nor what the possible consequences for us might have been.

Tapping the counter with a half-crown piece until the landlord reappeared, Dodger put in a request for another seven pints of HSB, the local Horndean Special Beer.

'I'll just tell the others to bring their glasses,' muttered Dodger. By now, the buzz had got around as to what the landlord was up to. Confirmation of this was made when one Pincher Martin, a budding lower-deck lawyer, his scheming mind working overtime as usual, whispered, 'Got that? I will count to three…' So, as he was topping up the final pint, the landlord was somewhat startled when, with full pints in their hands, the matelots who had been standing at the bar responded to Pincher reaching 'three' by slowly and deliberately turning their glasses upside down. Timed to perfection, these several upturned glasses, all of which had been topped up with HSB, slowly began slithering to the edge of the bar, assisted in their passage by the meniscus that had been created on that surface by the landlord's prize liquid. The sound of all that bitter cascading onto the wooden floor prompted the delighted locals to let out an almighty cheer as the duty watch hotfooted it to the rear exit whence they had come, leaving the landlord gobsmacked and, it has to be said, drenched by his overpriced brew.

'Cor, I wish I had a camera,' shouted the local gigolo.

'What a waste though,' retorted 'Benefit Pete'. Those two locals had taken special delight in the escapade.

'Shut up or get out,' said the landlord. He had spoken and he wasn't a very happy pixie.

Meanwhile, back at *Mercury*, the telephone was being answered by Chalky who began taking down the caller's rather scrambled message.

'Yes sir, I will sir. Maybe they are not from *Mercury*, sir? Now sir, sir, do please stop shouting and swearing, it really isn't going to help. Yes, your complaint will most certainly be investigated. Thank you, sir. Goodbye'.

With the inevitable ranting and raving out of the way, Chalky replaced the telephone receiver, had a little snigger to himself and continued reading his girlfriend's fruity letter for the umpteenth time. Meanwhile, and according to Chalky, during this otherwise quiet period, frantic muffled grunts and groans began emitting from the OOW's caboose, clearly audible through the thin wooden stud wall amidst faint 'shushings' that were just about audible between the peaks of exhaustion and delight.

We were, of course, continuing to make our hasty retreat from the pub, carving out a course back to the woods and following a plan that had previously been worked out 'just in case'. It took just nine minutes to run from the pub, through the woods to the boundary of Mercury's precincts and well within earshot of the camp's tannoy broadcasting system. Four minutes were allowed for musters from the time any broadcast requesting the same were made, owing to the expanse of the camp area. If, therefore, in the event we weren't able to respond in time with interrogation to follow, the practised and extremely well-rehearsed story was to be as follows:

'We were rounding up the pigs, sir, someone had opened the gate again.' This was not an uncommon occupation over any otherwise boring weekend duty; in fact, it had happened only the previous week when some pigs had strayed into the wardroom dining hall!

Following a break for a much-needed breather, Dusty Miller, scanning all before him, asked, 'Where's Taffy?' No Taffy. Ginger Rust said he had seen him alter course as everyone had bolted into the wood. We all shouted for him. 'Taff, Taff?' No answer. Lofty Short, all six feet four inches of him, a man who had been built like a rejected bean stick, then espied some movement in some nearby scrub, pointing to where a much bedraggled apparition could be heard clawing its way through the undergrowth, his sense of direction taken, no doubt, by the glaring southerly sun that shone into the undergrowth. The apparition was, by now, heard to be laughing its head off.

Before anyone had a chance to speak, said apparition, which was, of course, Taffy, blurted out the following story.

'As I was scarpering from the pub, I noticed two lily-white billy goats munching away at a bed of stinging nettles that were struggling to find some light in the back garden. I didn't take too kindly to the way that these lovely animals were restricted and chained up in such a small and dirty space, so I let them loose. The last thing that I remember was watching a large off-white tablecloth hanging from an apology for a clothes line, being rapidly reduced to fodder, pegs and all. I hate seeing animals tied up, it's cruel.'

Taffy was like that. Rumour had it that, following a good 'run ashore' with a couple of his mates on Barry Island in South Wales, he was alleged to have released a pair of king penguins that were destined for Newport zoo from their cages. The magistrate, in his summing up, had said it had been an irresponsible act by someone who should have known better and duly fined him two and sixpence. At that stage in proceedings, Taff then had the audacity to ask the arresting officer, with whom he was well acquainted (and who was currently holding him up) for a loan so that he could pay the fine. The night in a choice Welsh cell that followed soon brought this tough and hardened young man to his senses.

The following morning, reaching for one of his socks, Taffy withdrew a crumpled and stinking one-pound note to pay the policeman back with, saying, 'Put the change in the lifeboat box please, a few moons back they pulled me out of the oggin when I slipped off the gangway returning from a good run ashore in Singers' (Singapore). Meanwhile, the brown envelope that Taffy had been entrusted with by the clerk of the court to take back to his ship mysteriously became entangled with the flotsam and jetsam that was swilling around in Tiger Bay. His day in court, needless to say, made the local newspaper. But no one aboard his ship could read it as not one of them could read Welsh. Mind you, Taff couldn't either whenever he was stone cold sober. He wasn't in the least bit bothered about any of this though. He never was. His three good conduct badges were fixed on his arm with press studs, on and off his uniform like a pair of party's drawers!

At sea however, our lively Welshman was a great asset to his ship. Buffer, the chief bosun's mate, heavily relied upon Taffy if anything needed doing that was a little out of the ordinary or out of hours. Often, when neither sight or sound had been seen of him for a few hours, Taffy could be found lying horizontal in the buffers' store snoring his head off amidst a haze of fermenting rum that had been purloined, as suitable recompense for extra duties done, from the buffers' illicit rum bottle. He was, in all weathers, rain, sun or calm, a Welsh-speaking (in terms of expletives anyway) able seaman who was a joy to have on board. Ashore, however, well, that was a completely different kettle of fish. The lad from Barry Island could then be a bit of a liability. It was even rumoured that he could write the word 'police' in every conceivable language under the sun, so familiar was he with most of the world's law enforcement representatives – and that included Cantonese, which he was able to speak very fluently.

Whilst we were berthed in Malta, Taffy had managed, whilst on a spot of shore leave on Strait Street (Valletta's most well-known nightclub and bar area, known as 'the Gut' to English sailors), to get himself involved in something of an altercation and was arrested, only after having shown some resistance, by the naval shore patrol police. The morning after his arrest and, with his head still pounding with an almighty hangover, Taffy found himself on the receiving end of fourteen days' stoppage of leave after the captain had heard all about his latest little escapade. Rumour has it that, whilst telling his usual somewhat embroidered account of the punch-up he'd been involved in, one that had also involved some visiting sailors from the US Navy, Taff was said to have remarked, and in sharp contradiction to what the US Navy sailors would have claimed, that 'History dictates they are not the finest Navy in the world, are they Sir?'. The master-at-arms (MAA) who is always present at the captain's table during such hearings, relates that, upon hearing Taffy say this, the captain's response, spoken under his breath was, 'He's certainly right there.'

With the ship due to sail in four days' time, the captain instructed the MAA that Taffy's sentence was to start when it sailed, with the added warning that any more excess frivolity ashore would see Taffy end up at a detention centre that was rumoured to be a little like Alcatraz – less the birds! Mind you, this meant that his award of fourteen days' stoppage of leave was due to end at about the same time as the ship was in the vicinity of Gan, a tiny island that makes up part of the Maldives in the Indian Ocean. That meant that Taff would, in reality, lose no leave time at all. With the hearing at an end and Taffy now being ordered by the jaunty (MAA) to about turn and quick march, the captain added, pointing to the three good conduct badges that were held onto his uniform by press studs, 'Next time, we may have to borrow a couple of those again.'

***

Our otherwise peaceful life at HMS *Mercury* down in deepest Hampshire was disturbed, one dull and rather wet Monday morning, by an announcement on the tannoy that I couldn't help but take more than a passing interest in for the simple reason that, of the ten names that were read out for immediate muster, one of them was mine. The ten of us gathered together so quickly we arrived there five minutes before the nominated time – to be told that we had all volunteered for services in submarines.

'Transport will be leaving for HMS *Dolphin*, the submarine school at Gosport, at 1000 tomorrow morning.' And that was that. To add to our misery, next-of-kin forms were being handed out to each of us for swift completion.

You could, I promise you, have heard a pin drop. We were all stunned, completely and utterly stunned. One reason for that was the recent losses of the submarines *Affray* and *Truculent*, incidents that were, not surprisingly, at the forefront of our minds even before this rather sudden announcement. HMS *Affray* had set out on a simulated war mission in April 1951 with a reduced crew of 50 from the standard 61. Contact was lost a week later before, two months later, the wreck was found in a deep underwater valley in the English Channel.

HMS *Truculent* had been lost whilst it was returning to Sheerness in January 1950. It had recently had a refit at Chatham dockyard and was travelling through the Thames Estuary at night when it was involved in a collision with the Swedish oil tanker *Divina*. The impact of the collision left the two vessels locked together on the surface for a few seconds before *Truculent* broke away and sank. Many of the crew survived the incident and managed to escape, only to die in the freezing cold waters. *Truculent* itself was eventually salvaged and beached at Cheney Spit, a reminder to anyone who saw it there of the very real and constant dangers that you are putting yourself in as a crew member of a submarine, even in, as this case proved, the relatively 'safe' waters off the English coast and in this case within sight of land in the Thames Estuary.

So you can, perhaps, understand the reason for our concerns at being told we had all volunteered for the submarine service and that our naval lives on board one looked to be commencing, without any warning, within the next 24 hours. Mutterings of discontent soon began to circulate, claims that included, 'They can't do that' (they can); 'I didn't volunteer' (makes no difference) and 'Over my dead body'. All said with feeling. But the die was cast. We were going. And, just to make sure things didn't get too out of hand, a naval policeman (also known as a 'burley crusher') was left with us so that some kind of order was maintained. That's no surprise; I can understand why the Navy made that allowance. No one in their right mind would ever volunteer for service in submarines, despite the lucrative carrot of quite a bit of extra money. But that meant nothing to us; we could not believe we had been put in the situation we were now in. Taffy, who was one of the 'volunteers', made do with shouting a load of Welsh expletives and promptly made for the outside door only to be collared by another crusher who had joined his mate and one who instantly took a liking to our favourite Welshman's left lughole.

I was shaking like a leaf, thinking, 'How am I going to get out of this?' I was, and this is the absolute and honest truth, completely horrified. I would, at that moment, have rather been sent to the Royal Yacht and lost all hope of ever getting another promotion than end up in an iron coffin. Yes, those memories of *Affray* and *Truculent* and all the men that lost their lives serving on board them were very vivid in my mind. So that mind now began working overtime: there had to be some way out of this. The fact of the matter, as far as I was concerned, was that I was *not* going into submarines. And that was that. The other question that needed to be answered, of course, was why we had all, so suddenly and without explanation, been picked out for that service. Part of the answer there took me back to the boring time we'd spent minesweeping off the coast of Albania and the Corfu channel, from dawn to dusk; up and down, up and down, day after day after day after endless day. We were, at that time, sweeping for German-made mines that I believe had been laid by Albanian Navy after the Second World War was over. At around about the same time I'd enrolled on a correspondence course in order to learn Russian. This had been in 1951.

Now, as I read the classified signals and the occasional hints that were broadcast by the BBC's World Service, I had begun to realise that all the hallmarks of a military confrontation with Russia were looming very large on the horizon. In my eagerness to consider or do anything that might have got me away from doing service on submarines, I noticed, pinned up on the same notice board as the list of naval names of the new 'submarine volunteers', was another Admiralty Fleet Order (AFO) asking for telegraphists to volunteer for the Radio Warfare branch. Preference, the order went on, would be given to those willing to learn Russian. Well, here I was, the man who'd actually volunteered, two years earlier, to learn that very language. It seemed as if it might be a way out of being sent to submarines. Candidates, it added, should be able to read hand-operated Morse code at 25 words per minute.

I had little choice. This might just be my escape route. I immediately filled in the application request form, and then, quoting the AFO, handed it in. This had to be worth a try. Anything was better than having to serve in submarines, the very thought of which was now causing my stomach to churn in anticipation. No, this application had to work and I had to get the role with Radio Warfare. Because there was no way I was *ever* going into submarines.

Later on, we talked amongst ourselves whilst filling in our next-of-kin forms. I came to understand that Radio Warfare was a 'hush-hush' branch, the modern equivalent of the wartime 'Y' branch which had been an offshoot of a top-secret base at Bletchley Park during the war, later moving to Cheltenham. This was, and remains known as, Government

Communications Headquarters or GCHQ for short. It was here where 'Y' operators were responsible for intercepting Enigma Morse code signals that had been transmitted by the German U-boats ploughing the North Atlantic in their endeavours to curtail the passage of Allied merchant ships that were flying the red duster and supplying the war-ravaged USSR with essentials. Now, far from looking to protect Stalin's interests, the personnel at GCHQ were listening in to all Soviet radio traffic in an attempt to find out as much as they could about anything and everything that was happening in the Soviet Bloc.

The route to the Radio Warfare section was across the Droxford public road, one which effectively cut *Mercury* in half. This was known as North Camp and was a closed-off area surrounded by a high wire security fence that was guarded, day and night, by a sentry armed with a key to the six-foot-high entrance gate, a short stick and a telephone. Having made my hasty application, I now had to make myself known to Radio Warfare themselves. Once through the gate, for no reason whatsoever, I began to shake all over. It was a particularly eerie sensation, as if, somehow, my every move was being watched – as, unbeknownst to me, it was. I should add that, at that time, I had no idea that North Camp had been built over an ancient burial site. That was probably just as well. As I continued into the base, I came across a sign saying 'Office' with an accompanying arrow that was pointing to the right. It was there that I caught site of a chief petty officer (CPO) through the half-opened window of an old red-brick building, sat at a desk and watching, as he had been all along, my every move. Knocking on that office door, I entered the room to the echoes of a voice saying, 'Can't you read, lad?' In my frustration, I half pivoted around to see what he was referring to, tripped over the coir door mat and fell flat on my face to yet another well-observed witticism of 'You can't sleep here.' Things were going well.

'You'd better make yourself a cup of tea. Beasley, isn't it?'

'Yes,' I managed to blurt out.

'Take a seat, lad, and settle down. I'll make the tea. How many sugars?'

After numerous questions and two examination papers, I was called into the office of the officer in charge, a lieutenant commander who would, no doubt, be destined for a higher rank one day. More questions.

'Why do you want to join the Radio Warfare branch?' I couldn't very well say, even though it was the very reason I was sat there in front of him. The worst thing I could say would have been that it would get me out of having to serve on board submarines. I dithered a bit before eventually replying, 'Because I wanted to, sir.'

'To avoid being send to *Dolphin* for the submarine course, I suppose?'

'Not really, sir,' I lied, my body language effectively giving me away even as I stuttered out the reply.

Having passed the 25-words-per-minute Morse code test, I returned to the CPO's office.

'I see you've found your sea legs, Beasley. Sit down.'

A whole new range of questions followed.

'Any scars? Wear a ring, a watch? Any tattoos? Smoke, married, queer?' My answers to each of those questions having been in the negative, he went on, 'We don't want anyone being able to easily identify you, do we?'

'No... no, chief.'

'We stutter a bit, do we? Nerves, lad, nerves. Just calm down, we won't eat you, not alive anyway.'

I was, little by little and systematically, becoming more and more at ease in this new and totally, for me, unexpected, environment; still baffled, I have to admit, as to what I was letting myself in for.

'Born in 1933. Twenty-one then, just a sprog. Come to think of it, a 1933 penny is the only one missing from my collection. If you find one, I'll give you a crisp white fiver for it I will.'

'I bet you will,' I thought. 'I bet you will.'

Leaning back in his well-worn armchair and eyeing me up and down as if there was no tomorrow, the CPO went on.

'Next Thursday, you will be starting a conversion course along with several other telegraphists. You will muster outside this office at 0830 in smart working dress, polished boots and armed with a couple of sharp pencils. These...' he muttered, handing me a Blue Station card, '... are like gold dust. This is your passport to escape all *Mercury* duties.'

Station cards were a form of identity.

'You now come under me for everything. I mean everything. Leave, discipline, grandma dying, girlfriend up the duff. I want to know everything. If I don't, I'll soon find out. Don't lose that card, there are those who would give a few weeks of tot to get their hands on one of these.'

That advice turned out to be very true.

'How well you do on the conversion course, which lasts at least ten exhausting weeks, determines whether you keep the blue card or not. If you fail, I have little doubt that your next stop will be the submarine school. And we don't want that, do we?'

No, 'we' most certainly did not. But the CPO hadn't finished yet.

'Every other Friday you will be examined in the previous week's work with a wash-up (review meeting) the following Monday. You can leave now, you've just about time to get your tot. I don't want to see or hear from you until Thursday. My name is Chief Petty Officer Telegraphist (Special) Shade. You will then be free to come and see me whenever you wish, providing it's before 1130, after which time I cannot be held responsible for my actions. Incidentally, I detest being called Chief, my birth certificate confirms I'm not a Red Indian and I do not, nor have I ever, worn feathers. Clear?'

'Yes Chief Telegraphist Shade,' I shakily replied. Where had I heard that before? As I opened the door to leave, Chief Telegraphist Shade raised his voice and added, 'One other thing, lad. If you ever cackle about anything you see or do in this place, I will find out. Your feet won't touch the deck until the cell door slams behind you and the key gets thrown overboard. Clear?'

'Yes, Chief Petty Officer Shade.'

'Carry on.'

Returning to the mess for my tot and dinner, I couldn't believe how things had worked out in my favour. A few hours previously, I was in the throes of being sent to *Dolphin* as a coerced 'volunteer' for submarines. As for Chief Telegraphist Shade, there was one thing I couldn't work out about him. And that was why he didn't want to be disturbed after 1130. I soon found out, the hard way: his 'tot time' was 1130!

***

The next ten weeks were strenuous and very tiring. The entire course was oriented around Russian SIGINT (signal intelligence) and ELINT (electronic intelligence). Normal hours for instruction sessions went out of the window as the course progressed. Russian communication procedures differed greatly from our own and were, in my view, easier to understand. Reading live Russian Morse code circuits means sessions starting at 2000 and lasting all night and well into the morning. Their local communications net used low frequencies, generally in the waveband 1200 kcs to 3000 kcs, which was much the same as the range we used and, I might add, not unlike that used by some other countries as well.

At night, when the ionosphere lowers, radio ground waves on those frequencies travel much further. It was not unusual, therefore, to pick up transmissions from such far flung places as Tashkent, Tbilisi, Vladivostok, Irkutsk, Novosibirsk, Baku and Moskva to name a few, locations spread out over many thousands of miles and several different time zones. The Russian submarine broadcast service, UBS, transmitting from the North Ural mountains on 23 kcs, was on a par with our own submarine broadcast, GBR, which transmitted from Rugby on 16 kcs.

Both these frequencies could be received in many parts of the world by submarines lurking out of sight just below the surface. Towards the end of the original expected ten-week course, the syllabus entered into the largely unknown world of Russian radars, guidance systems and ELINT. This highly absorbing and intense subject fascinated me and gathered my sole interest. I was now hoping that my original request to take a Russian language course to become a linguist had been forgotten. Unfortunately, it had not, as you will shortly see.

This was the early 1950s, a time when relations with Russia and its satellite states were about as low as they could get. I found this difficult to get my head around; after all, less than ten years previously, the Allies had been protecting convoys carrying supplies to the northern Russian ports from the full destructive resources of Admiral Karl Dönitz's German U-boat packs that were lying in wait, hidden and ready to strike, under the surface of the seas. Hundreds of men from the Royal Navy and the Merchant Navy were lost in the tempestuous North Atlantic and Arctic Oceans as well as the notorious Barents Sea (located off the northern coasts of Norway and Russia and divided between Norwegian and Russian territorial waters); men and ships, all of whom were serving and dying in the cause of supporting the Russian people and armed forces. Times had changed suddenly and very swiftly, however, as we were now on the brink of war against our former ally, a fact that very few people at the time realised. Yet it was partly due to the brave seamen who crewed those often worn-out ships that the battle for Stalingrad had eventually ended in victory for Russia's tired yet very determined resistance.

The 'Y' branch, forerunner of the Radio Warfare branch, was accountable for detecting and positioning the U-boats by 'huffduff' (HFDF, or high frequency direction finding). This was the form of Morse code transmission on a high-frequency wavelength that provided the intercepted Enigma codes for Alan Turing's[1] extremely clever team of ladies who were working in Hut 8 of Bletchley Park to decode. When this happened, the appendix on the top and bottom of all our paperwork was, at a stroke, amended from TOP SECRET to TOP SECRET UK EYES ONLY. Whilst on that subject I should add that another classification which appeared, albeit not very often, was TOP SECRET BURN BEFORE READING!

I was still hoping that my request to take a Russian language course had been forgotten. This had not been the case and, as a result, the dreaded day had arrived that saw me ushered into a stark, cold room to sit before an interview panel for assessment as to my suitability to undertake a Russian language course at RAF Pucklehurst. I entered the damp and musty classroom before being told by an officer, would you believe, of the junior service, to sit and speak only when I was spoken to. What a good introduction for me to the RAF that was! Directly to my front sat five men, all of whom seemed to be squatting on unstable wooden chairs behind two equally wobbly trestle tables that had been pushed together.

---

1 An English computer scientist, Turing worked for the Government Code and Cypher School (GC&CS) at Bletchley Park where he devised a number of techniques for speeding up the breaking of German ciphers, including improvements to the pre-war Polish bombe method, an electromechanical machine that could find settings for the famous Enigma machine.

To my immediate right was a short, bald-headed and kindly looking man from GCHQ. He was flanked by two Royal Navy instructor officers. To my left, a pompous-looking RAF squadron leader, presumably also an instructor, sat. Next to him was another officer from the Royal Navy, an instructor lieutenant. Right from the off, it seemed to me that the RAF officer was in charge, with my immediate thought in response being, 'How can I nudge myself out of this?' I now wanted to take that Russian language course, previously so appealing, like I wanted a hole in the head.

Perched on a rickety old chair and not daring to move in case it squeaked, I waited for my inquisition to begin, which it did after the quintet in front of me had eyed me up and down most deliberately as if I had leprosy or some other equally horrific wasting disease. Then they started.

'What do you think of present world affairs?'

'Where did you go to school?'

'What qualifications have you achieved?'

'What do your mother and father do?'

To this last question, I replied that they both worked for Harold Macmillan MP at Gosses Farm in Birch Grove as his cook and head gamekeeper respectively. My answer made them all briefly look at one another before continuing their stream of never-ending questions, something which, gradually, was making me more and more irritated as the minutes ticked away. It didn't help that, every time I crossed my legs or made even the slightest move, the chair creaked, instantly drawing the attention of one of the RAF officers. I was beginning to grow weary of all this. What time was it? The classroom clock showed 2359. 'I wish it were midnight...', I thought, '... as that would mean I wouldn't have to be in this godforsaken place'. Yet the interview went on and on for quite a bit longer. Eventually though, after what seemed an eternity, the quiet gentleman from GCHQ said, 'Thank you, please wait outside.' I left the room and paced up and down the freezing corridor outside, hoping beyond hope that I wasn't going to be selected to take the linguist course as I felt I had well and truly now found my niche in ELINT and didn't want to leave.

'Beasley!' My name echoed down and around that draughty corridor. The junior service officer had once again spoken. I went back in and, after closing the door, was about to sit down when that very same officer said, in a tone that came across in the same frightening manner to you as the sound, or rather lack of same, when the engine on a doodlebug packs up. 'I will tell you when to sit!' He was now beginning to rub me up the wrong way, noisy young thing from the most junior of all the services. I then sat and listened as every member of the board, except the noisy young thing, gave their opinion as to my suitability to attend a Russian linguist course. And, to be very honest with you, I was extremely flattered. In fact, as I sat there listening to them, my head began to swell and I started to believe that all this praise, as welcome as it was, would mean that I was about to be selected. 'Please,' I was hoping, 'please say that I am unsuitable.'

'Stop daydreaming and pay attention!' It was he who must be obeyed, the irritating RAF officer again. He then added, 'You are unsuitable. We have detected a stutter. You may leave.' How dare he, a man who was nothing more than a jumped-up school teacher and one who was, in addition to that, wearing a most ill-fitting RAF uniform, speak to me like that? I immediately stood up, feeling the pins and needles in both of my legs as I did so. Attempting at least a smartish about-turn, I tripped over my chair in one precise movement, smashing it to pieces in the process of falling. Picking myself up off the deck and still feeling a little off balance as I did so, I inclined my head to one side as I collided with the door, muttering calmly but distinctly, 'Surely some of the 200 million Russians out there stutter?' The sound of sniggering followed as, thankfully, I left the cold and distinctly inhospitable room.

With my routine now uninterrupted, I found myself, within a few weeks, one of a handful of highly trained ELINT operators specialising in Russian radar and tracking systems, both of which were constantly being updated. I loved every minute of it. Maybe not quite so much, mind you, when I was rolling my guts out in a force ten gale on board one of the fishery protection minesweepers, namely *Truelove*, *Mariner* and *Pickle*, as we sailed off the northern Norwegian coast capturing signals emanating from the Russian Northern Fleet. Keeping watch in an open all-weather bridge with no covering whatsoever is arduous enough but, when you're constantly having to chip ice from your eyebrows, nose, ears and fingers, it all makes life just that little bit more irksome. On such trips, the deck would be icy all the time and we often had to tie ourselves to anything that didn't move for the sake of our safety. That was all very well. But then attempting to untie oneself using frozen fingers was an art that I never seriously accomplished. To this day, my fingers and toes visibly confirm the long-term effects of frostbite all those years ago.

Most of the equipment we used was put together by ourselves in something of a Heath Robinson style. But, although it was basic, it worked and it worked well. Secreted within a pair of heavy-duty cruiser binoculars, replacing the eye pieces, were wave guides: 'S' band to the left and 'X' band to the right, with both set at 45 degrees for horizontal and vertical polarisation radars as it was otherwise difficult to differentiate between the two polarisations due to the rolling of the ship. Co-axial leads ran from each eye piece across our shoulders to recording machines that were nestled under blankets and canvas sheets nearby. The only real problem we had with our imaginatively conceived equipment was that, whenever we were close to the ships that were transmitting radar, Russian sailors, watching through their own high-powered binoculars, couldn't fail to see, as they were watching us, that we were 'watching' them with our eyes above the eye pieces.

Another piece of radar intercept equipment used was a fixed scanning flipping device for interception of aircraft using 'X' band. The theory was that, whenever we detected a target, the linguist down below in his nice warm office would then be able to search for any 'ship to air' voice communications and, in doing so, tie up Russian operational capacity. We attempted this just the once but failed miserably due to the ever-present ice and rolling of the ship. Little did we know at the time that these little jaunts with the Fishery Protection Squadron, in which we often witnessed our trawlers being intimidated by the Icelandic Navy, were an inkling of some much more serious confrontations[2] to come.

---

2 The author is referring to the Cod Wars, a series of confrontations between the United Kingdom and Iceland on fishing rights in the North Atlantic that took place, with frequent skirmishes between ships of both nations, from the late 1940s until 1976.

Our main causes of concern whenever we were at sea on these operations were mail, provisions and fuel. So, whenever possible, we called into the Norwegian port of Tromsø which is the third largest city north of the Arctic Circle. It's an extremely friendly place, picturesque too, as it is nestled between peaks that are adorned with ice and snow. It was a convenient stopping-off place for fishery protection minesweepers to land and collect mail as well as taking on fresh supplies of fuel and water, milk, fruit and green vegetables. The Norwegians were always incredibly welcoming and courteous to us although I have to say that their onion beer was terrible!

On one occasion, as we were leaving Tromsø Post Office, having collected some incoming mail, an English deep-sea fisherman out of Kingston-upon-Hull asked us if we would take some of their letters for delivery back home as the mail situation otherwise was very unreliable, expensive, and often took several weeks to arrive. With a little arm-twisting, we agreed to do this. In return, we were given several boxes of delicious filleted cod and haddock, the like of which I have, to this day, never tasted. The pusser (purser) on board HMS *Pickle* paid for the couple of dozen letters or so at a cost of a penny-halfpenny each – and that was by airmail! These letters were mixed with our own ship's mail and addressed to BFPO Ships in London. We, meanwhile, were set to sail for the delights of Bear Island, some two hundred miles further north.

During one four-day stopover in Tromsø, a dozen or so crew from HMS *Truelove*, including our team of four, were invited by the Norwegian Navy to go on a skiing adventure. All equipment, we were told, including the appropriate clothing, would be provided for us. What we weren't told was that the piste was the upturned hull of the German pocket battleship *Tirpitz,* sunk in November 1944 after RAF Lancaster bombers equipped with 12,000-pound 'Tallboy' bombs scored two direct hits. We all had a marvellous time on a day that was only slightly marred by one, yes, just the one, broken bone. Sometime after that, what turned out to be our final farewell to Tromsø came when all four of our team that had joined from *Mercury* 'borrowed' a stuffed polar bear from its place outside the fur shop at the top of the hill which led down to the pier head. Releasing the bear from its shackles, we all took turns in riding it, much to the amusement of the watching local fishermen. Obviously the onion beer was a little stronger than we had been led to think. Little did we know, in those carefree days, that we would soon be passing Tromsø en route to more enlightening places east of Honningsvåg (the northernmost city in Norway, which lies on the western edge of the notorious Barents Sea) in a vastly different mode of travel.

Several of my oppos portrayed here and in the next chapter have since crossed over the Styx. We were all, at that time, single and roughly the same age, which would have been one of the reasons for our selection in the first place. The Admiralty had justification for this.

It's not too difficult to fathom why.

CHAPTER 5

The Art of Radar

'Whatever we knew about the certain characteristics of anything was highly likely to be known by others also, a philosophy that I always tried to instil into my students later in my career. If we know it, they know it.'

For almost a week, the coming and going of staff cars had been a regular occurrence at HMS *Mercury*. Many of these cars were replete with important-looking men, all of whom were clasping official briefcases, which were, more often than not, shackled to their wrists. These men all had one other thing in common: they were the attendees of meetings that were being held in our small and somewhat antiquated Radio Warfare specialist unit in HMS *Mercury*'s North Camp. These visitors, it was soon worked out by those with an ever-watchful eye and enquiring mind, were from GCHQ in Cheltenham.

A dozen or so students, myself included, were in the continued process of being taught the sparsely known characteristics of electronic intelligence and signal intelligence. I'd already been able to put some of my training into practice whilst under secondment, with three *Mercury* colleagues, to the fisheries protection team as detailed in the previous chapter. Now, back at *Mercury*, we were only too well aware of how the Cold War was, to coin a phrase, 'hotting up', and that a future military confrontation with Russia, a country that had been our ally only a decade previously, was looking more and more likely.

The phrase 'Cold War' was first used by the English author George Orwell, famous, of course, for such books as *Animal Farm* and *1984*. He wrote an article in 1945 which predicted a forthcoming nuclear stalemate between 'two or three monstrous super-states, each possessed of a weapon by which millions of people can be wiped out in a few seconds', christening this state of affairs the 'Cold War'. This term was carefully noted by the American financier and presidential advisor Bernard Baruch, who used it in a speech he made at the State House in Columbia, South Carolina, two years later.

A new and terrifying phrase had entered the political lexicon.

Britain's role in proceedings would, of course, have been to back the United States in any and all actions that would either be taken or considered in response to the very real threat of an expansionist USSR and the spectre of communism. Churchill had, throughout the Second World War, looked to co-operate with and support Stalin but that was just a means to an end. Churchill despised communism and knew, deep down, that a new world conflict between the capitalist west and communist east was increasingly likely. This might even have been a war that had broken out only a few years or even months after the previous conflict had ended and may well have done if so many of the potential participants, notably the USSR, hadn't needed to rebuild their social and military infrastructures from 1945 onwards.

One intriguing argument states that the origins of the Cold War can be traced all the way back to Churchill, whose belligerent attitude towards the USSR was picked up on and even admired by US President Harry Truman as he took office in April 1945. Churchill certainly added a phrase of his own to the dictionary when, in 1946, he gave a speech at Westminster College in Fulton, Missouri, saying, 'From Stettin in the Baltic to Trieste in the Adriatic, an iron curtain has descended across the Continent. Behind that line lie all the capitals of the ancient states of Central and Eastern Europe. Warsaw, Berlin, Prague, Vienna, Budapest, Belgrade, Bucharest and Sofia, all these famous cities and the populations around them lie in what I must call the Soviet sphere, and all are subject in one form or another, not only to Soviet influence but to a very high and, in many cases, increasing measure of control from Moscow.'

It was a speech that Churchill had named 'The Sinews of Peace' and, if its intention had been to alternately flatter and terrify Great Britain's biggest ally, then it succeeded. Truman may well have had every intention of adopting a similarly aggressive stance against the USSR but he and most of the western world now seemed to have every reason to do so after taking in Churchill's words. Nazism had been thwarted but, in that victory, the seeds of a far greater threat to the world had duly been sown. And they were ripening with great haste.

The USA and its allies had been deeply committed to doing all they could to prevent the growth of communism ever since. Not through military means, at least not those which meant direct conflict. No, the methods that had been utilised ever since Churchill had raised the stakes by referring to the 'Iron Curtain' had been strictly covert, with both sides doing their level best to find out what the other was doing without, crucially, being caught in the act. We knew they were spying on us and they knew we were spying on them. Much of the activity in Britain focused on GCHQ, and now where the constant comings and goings of staff cars at HMS *Mercury* were a symptom of a change of policy within the unit at North Camp that included students being selected for possible operations in the near future, the details of which were presently unknown. Prior to that, operations had been known and planned well in advance and were generally of a short duration, perhaps some two to three weeks. Permanent attachments, on the other hand, were a lot longer in duration and involved postings to places like Germany, Cyprus, Hong Kong and Ascension Island, some of which would mean those taking up the postings would be accompanied by their families for periods that might have been for as long as two years.

Many of the selected few spent what free time they did have in the camp's squash courts, hammering out their frustrations on the small black balls, often doing so with such energetic vehemence that they broke their racquets. Others took out their anger at whatever injustice they perceived had been put upon them by attending the pistol and rifle ranges with Chief Gunnery Instructor 'Corny Cornelius'. He was a full-blooded gunnery man with a beard worthy of any make-up artist plus three rows of medal ribbons that he had earned over both world wars. Corny appeared, on first impressions, to be a strikingly aggressive man but the reverse was true. In reality, he was as soft as a gulp of Navy net rum, that beloved daily tot that disappeared forever in July 1970.

Our instructors had, over a period of a few weeks, been focusing on known intelligence data associated with what we were picking up from Russian radar. In hindsight, that was precious little. On other occasions, we concentrated on Russian low frequency Morse code nets and voice channels, access to which would be enhanced by the dropping ionosphere in the early hours. All in all, then, our focus and daily duties were forever subject to change but, for all that, the one thing that never changed was the fact that we would always be hard at work throughout the night, every night, and into the early hours of the following day. During this time, the area around our secret unit was blissfully quiet and away from prying eyes and sensitive ears. Much of this peace and quiet was due to the fact that the Radio Warfare Unit was bounded on two sides by small hedgerows, together with numerous fields, all of which were abundant with cattle and sheep. North Camp was divided from the main camp by a public road and, from time to time, we'd hear of incidents involving possible intruders who would, on every occasion, be eagerly investigated by the lone guard on the gate of the North Camp, armed, as he always was, with a short stick and a torch!

Up to now, all of the students, myself included, who were undergoing tuition, had been to sea on one of the fleet's fishery protection minesweepers, HMS *Truelove*, HMS *Pickle* or HMS *Mariner*. The hope was, and it was often more hope than expectation, that we would be able to snatch some ELINT emissions from the Russian warships that were always out of visual range, exercising, as they would, in either the North Atlantic or off the western and northern coasts of Norway. These exercises were, however, a known quantity and you pretty much knew what you'd be doing and for how long. Those increasingly frequent visits from the men at GCHQ were now serving to make us realise that, one way or the other, the old and familiar parameters of the Cold War were changing as was the role we might be expected to play in it and that we might, with little or no warning, end up being selected for a mission which might not even have been thought of just a few short weeks earlier.

That is when, rightfully, you might have spent a little bit of time genuinely worrying about your future welfare.

Eventually I found myself, along with six other students, being selected for one of these seemingly cobbled-together missions. We were, upon selection, advised to write six weeks' worth of letters to our loved ones which was, to say the least, a little bit unusual. Writing letters in such a way is a bit like talking to yourself, after a while, as you are not able to say what you have been up to, so repetition becomes unavoidable. There is also, of course, the added problem of having no mail to answer. So it all becomes rather frustrating with the noise of tearing paper and the sound of it being crumpled up and thrown at the nearest waste paper basket frequently heard. An additional oddity was that the likely candidates for such covert operations were all asked if they had any medical or dental problems and if their next-of-kin forms were in date. These are the sort of questions that can't really be asked without eliciting some sort of concern in the mind of the recipient. We later found out, in relation to this, that sending a group of men from the Radio Warfare unit en masse for medical and dental treatments might have compromised the unit's secret intentions although, personally, I doubt if that would have been the case as all of these unusual happenings had never taken place before, whatever the nature of the eventual operation that followed.

Understandably, therefore, buzzes were rife. What was happening, what might be happening, where were we going, why and for how long? If you've just been asked to write six weeks' worth of letters, a request that precluded any hope of sending or receiving some for that period of time, it can stir up the internal feelings of any matelot and, because of this, the related anguish and outrageous speculation was rife. Needless to say, the longer this situation continued, the worse the associated torment became. Three of 'our' seven were courting Wrens (members of the Women's Royal Naval Service) to whom they found it much more difficult to write long-term letters. Another member of the possible seven was Taffy, who was set to be the best man at our wedding. But sorting out a date for that was now proving to be tantalisingly awkward. How *do* you tell a girlfriend, someone who you write to three or four times a week as well as telephoning at least once, that you are going away for six or so weeks but have no idea where you might be going and won't be able to send or receive any mail in that time? What might reasonably go through her mind at that time? We were all, as the weeks dragged on, finding it more and more difficult to understand why this particular operation was so much more hush-hush than any of the previous ones. It really was like tiptoeing on eggshells.

***

The Cold War, as I have already explained, was continuously escalating and had been since 1947, something that the general public or even the vast majority of our armed services, including senior officers, were completely oblivious to as the 'need to know' maxim had been instilled into the minds of everyone. Under normal circumstances, the sort of buzzes that we had become familiar with soon revealed what they were all about, where we'd be going and for what purpose; however, for this one, there hadn't been even the slightest hint of a leak – and if there had, we would have very quickly known about it.

The only information going around at the time that seemed to have any worthiness seemed to concern Russian ELINT, which had been hammered into us time and time again in the past few weeks. We were repeatedly reminded of the characteristics of Russian radars until the sounds they made were engraved upon our minds and ears. Our progress was made all the more difficult by what was considered to be suspect information. Our allies frequently supplied us with tape recordings they had made of Russian radar traffic but they were so often misleading or erroneous that we eventually decided to ignore them.

Almost from the start of the buzz, the information, dodgy or good, that we were receiving, had its subject headings changed to TOP SECRET UK EYES ONLY. Our task, as always, was to find out as much information as we could and as fast as we could. It wasn't always easy. ELINT characteristics and the information they contain within the actual radar signal is a subject that is extremely difficult to teach, especially if, as we were at the time, you were constantly in receipt of limited or even false information. It also required specialist equipment. A radar pulse travels at the speed of light which is 186,000 miles per second, or, as we are in nautical mode for this book, 162,000 nautical miles per second.

Experience and, in particular, common sense is the safest and only way to describe ELINT. The latter, of course, is something that you either have or you do not, irrespective of your social or educational background. One known fact about Russian radars, however, was their use of an AC frequency of sixty cycles. Unfortunately, it is also the frequency used by the USA as well as some other countries, so reading and deciphering it is never as easy as 'just' tuning into 60 cycles and concluding that it must be Russian in origin. British radars, on the other hand, operate on 50 cycles. The first 'squeak' of a radar intercept is what determines its cycle.

The RAF did, of course, use a form of radar with some success during the Second World War by using masts that were erected along the southern coast of England and under the path of German aircraft. Later in the war, the RAF aircraft were fitted with what we now know as basic radar which, despite its simplicity, proved to be a great help. This was only the start of the whole evolutionary progress with regard to the technology that eventually led to what today's technicians have available to them, a clear example, back in the early 1940s, of 'from little acorns, grow big trees'.

One of these stations was referred to as RAF St Eval, which was a strategic station for RAF Coastal Command situated on the Cornish coast. It had multiple roles but was, primarily, used to provide anti-sub-marine and anti-shipping patrols off the south-west coast. The station also provided aircraft that were used for photographic reconnaissance missions, meteorological flights, convoy patrols, air-sea rescue missions and for the protection of the airfield from Luftwaffe raids. Cornwall might have seemed fairly remote as far as the war was concerned but, make no mistake: that station was the proverbial hive of activity as were all of its peers stretching up and away eastwards to Dover and its famous white cliffs.

That war was still a relatively recent memory for most. But both the stakes and the enemy had changed, for it was now Soviet transmissions and military activity that we were interested in. But you had to know what you were listening to and also, at the same time, be aware that what you were doing in order to do so was going to be heard by others.

Which is why one of the things our instructor was always telling us is that whatever we knew about the certain characteristics of anything we listened into or even saw, this was also highly likely to be known by others also. So, although our work was deemed to be 'Top Secret', the truth of the matter was probably that no one had any secrets really, as you'd be extremely unlikely to be able to keep them from friend and foe alike. This was a philosophy that I always tried to instil into my students later in my career. If we know it, they know it.

Our primary task was to establish what information was contained within differing types of Russian radar transmissions which, hopefully, supplied information about the purpose that radar was being used for. To be able to say, with confidence, that 'such and such' a radar is fitted onto a particular type of ship is a lot easier said than done. This was the information that GCHQ were crying out for, the confirmation of information obtained by intelligence sources by positive proof. The interception of any radar pulse provides, within microseconds, a vast amount of information, often indicating the role that radar is playing on that particular ship. But even when a radar transmission is positively matched to a rotating aerial from that ship, it's only the initial analysis that has been done.

The primary use of 'X' band, a high-frequency short-range radar is, for example, for navigational purposes. But even that carries a multitude of possible scenarios. 'X' band operates on a higher frequency than 'S' band, for example, which is used for a number of differing roles including height finding, gunnery, missile control, air defence and the like. So whilst we can reasonably hope to ascertain what a particular ship might be by listening into its radar signal, nothing, back then, beat having an actual physical close encounter with one – and by that, I really mean close. That was something I would, ultimately, have myself and one that was far too close to call.

As for a more general example, however, well, you wouldn't want to get too close to one of the Soviet's Kotlin-class destroyers. And we knew a fair bit about them. They were known, by the Soviets, as 'Project 56' or '*Spokoinyy*', which translates as 'tranquil'. Between 1955 and 1958, 27 of these were built as a smaller version of the *Neustrashimy*-class destroyers –

and they packed a punch with plenty of armament and a top speed that wasn't far off 40 knots. If you were careless enough to get within visual or even radar range of one of them, then you'd be in trouble. So stealth was very much the watchword when it came to keeping an eye on these ships as you'd still need to get close enough to detect the role of its radar, one purpose of which, in the case of the Kotlin ships, was to detect periscopes. Then there were the *Sverdlov*-class cruisers. These were deemed to be enough of a potential threat to justify the Royal Navy increasing its number of operational ships in the North Atlantic as well as introducing the Buccaneer strike aircraft, designed to operate off aircraft carriers and more than capable of attacking the *Sverdlov* ships whilst remaining out of reach of their guns.

Little inspires technological advancement more than war or the threat of the same and the presence of those ships had led to the MOD upping its game with that particular aircraft. And, with their fondness for bean counting[1], that new aircraft made a lot of sense as far as the bosses were concerned, for, rather than them having to practically rebuild the fleet in order to cope with the growing threat from the Soviet Navy, especially the *Sverdlov*-type cruisers, they could use the Buccaneer to attack them using conventional weapons or, if things were not looking too good, a bomb that included a nuclear warhead. The Buccaneer was an ideal aircraft for this sort of operation as it was able to approach enemy shipping at low altitudes beneath the cruisers' radar horizon. This was, of course, all very well if you needed to get in quick and try to sink the enemy before getting out again. But it wasn't a lot of good if you wanted to have a good look at or even a listen for an enemy ship whilst, of course, not being detected yourself.

During the mid-1950s, one-thousand-ton British submarines known as 'Super T' boats were the only surveillance options available for the type of close-quarter encounters required with such Russian vessels in order to capture the sort of information that GCHQ so desperately required. It goes without saying that such actions are extremely dangerous

---

1 Bean counting or bean counters – bureaucrats obsessed with saving money with, at times, a reckless disregard for the potential outcome of such a policy.

and bordering upon the suicidal. Yet the intricacies of reading and trying to 'translate' myriad radar systems were, for us, so complex and involved so many different possibilities that, if accurate information was needed, then we needed to get up close and personal to the ships in question. As time went by, British, American and Russian submarines of many thousands of tons undertook numerous covert operations in order to get this sort of information. These were vessels that could employ different methods of reading and detection as well as offering greater manoeuvrability but, for all that, they and their collective efforts cannot be compared with those British 'Super T' boats such as HMS *Totem* and HMS *Turpin*, ships that specialised in visual encounters, and which, if it had not been for the skills of their commanders, may well have ended up as another sad statistic along with the likes of HMS *Thetis, Truculent, Affray, Sidon* and, dare I say it, the Hull-based trawler *Gaul*. This ship was famously lost in 1974 whilst, according to rumour, on a Cold War spying mission, a claim that has since been denied at government level.

Every electronic transmission, be it radar or otherwise, displays its own fingerprint which, in turn, can identify a specific ship or even a particular operator. It also cannot be ruled out that a known radar's characteristics can be changed at the touch of a button, throwing ELINT computerised information previously thought of as proven into some turmoil. If in doubt, therefore, throw it out and start again. One can never rely specifically on data obtained using computers as, for numerous reasons, data can be difficult to interpret, no matter how it is gathered. You have no choice but to tread carefully at all times as radar and radio transmitters can be changed at will and computers can, and often do, display misleading information that can result in cataclysmic consequences.

One of these was the potential for inaccurate radar information leading to a collision between two submarines. This happened on more than one occasion. Back in 1974, the SSBN *James Madison* (an American ballistic nuclear submarine) armed with sixteen Poseidon nuclear missiles was heading out of the US naval base at Holy Loch in Scotland. But it was to be anything but a standard patrol, for, not long after leaving the port, it hit an unidentified Soviet submarine that had been sent into British waters in order to follow it. This was deemed so serious an incident that, despite the fact it took place relatively close to the British coast, the US administration at the time ordered that it be immediately covered up. It was and remained a secret for nearly fifty years.

The communiqué that American national security advisor sent to Henry Kissinger, then the US secretary of state under President Gerald Ford, was brief and to the point.

> Have just received word from the Pentagon that one of our Poseidon submarines has just collided with a Soviet Submarine.
>
> The SSBN James Madison was departing Holy Loch to take up station when it collided with a Soviet submarine waiting outside the port to take up trail.
>
> Both submarines surfaced and the Soviet boat subsequently submerged again. There is no report yet of the extent of damage. Will keep you posted.

'Will keep you posted'. It sounds as if the two of them are trying to arrange their weekly game of squash. Can you even begin to comprehend the thoughts that might have been going through the heads of the crews of both ships as the realisation of what had just happened dawned, violently, on them? The US ship was carrying sixteen nuclear missiles. Now they wouldn't have been armed so it was unlikely that they would have exploded as a result of the collision. But then you'd have thought it very likely that two submarines, both equipped with, for the time, state-of-the-art radar and detection systems, might just have been able to avoid hitting one another.

The CIA did its best to keep the incident under wraps but it wasn't long before both the *Washington Post* and the *National Intelligence Daily* got wind of the story and made it public with claims that were immediately, of course, denied.

And, whilst the chances of the *James Madison*'s nuclear payload (and/or that of the Soviet submarine) detonating en masse was slight, there was a far greater chance that either side might have interpreted the collision as an attack by their opposite number. What might have happened as a result of that? Then there was the possibility that both submarines might have capsized and gone to the bottom with not only an enormous loss of life on both sides but the prospect of a couple of 'hot' nuclear reactors left in relatively shallow water off the British coast, not to mention both ships' weapons. And here's another thing: how happy do you think the Soviets would have been to have lost a submarine in enemy waters, there for NATO forces to explore and reverse engineer?

You can be certain that would not have been allowed to happen.

Fortunately for humanity, the captains of both ships must have swiftly realised that the collision was not a result of hostile intent and, after the briefest of visual contacts, the Soviet submarine slunk off back to its secret base. I wonder what happened to its captain though, when he eventually got his crippled ship home again.

Electronic intelligence gathered from military aircraft and warships throughout the world is of vital importance. This became apparent during the Falklands War in 1982. Prior to this conflict, the emphasis when gathering information tended to be languages and signal intelligence, SIGINT, rather than ELINT, the electronic intelligence. This was brought home when it immediately became apparent that the Argentine Air Force were using French radars, missiles, aircraft, equipment and knowledge, which meant they were able to successfully detect and take out a Royal Navy destroyer, in this case HMS *Sheffield,* which was hit and crippled by a French-made Exocet missile. Such a possibility should, I believe, have been known and prepared for during the British task forces' eight-thousand-mile dash south in order to engage in this conflict. Even if it had been, then it was not, for me, done in a serious enough manner. Numerous comments about this ended up being made to me by some Electronic Warfare specialists which backed up my belief that, from the mid-1960s onwards, far too much emphasis was placed on teaching Russian and other languages, with ELINT being shoved into the background or not even mentioned; the final decision and priorities depended on which persuasion the officer in charge of the Electronic Warfare branch at HMS *Mercury* favoured. Since naval officers didn't, in the main, care too much about ELINT, wardroom talk was much more favourable when it came to discussing Russian, with SIGINT, it would seem, having their collective egos massaged whenever talk turned to discussing learning languages. Certain individual specialists in the

ELINT field would even be told to keep their mouths shut whenever they made a suggestion.

You can never have too much intelligence on an enemy: its men, its ships, its aircraft, anything at all. And it was for this reason and this reason alone that I chose the electronic intelligence route. Radars can be altered or even physically changed to use different characteristics which could spell danger if the information on a database is strictly adhered to. This is where experience and common sense play an integral part in knowing your subject. And this was what I was able to offer.

Eventually, and after what seemed a lifetime, all seven of the Radio Warfare students selected several weeks previously were called for interview. Four were eventually chosen from that seven, two of which were myself and Taffy. Yet, even at this stage, no mention at all was made of our destination or even our form of transport. Everything remained, just as it had been from the very start of the buzz, a complete mystery. All we were told, in the end, was that we were to pack a light hold-all with a few changes of underwear, socks, working dress and other basics, such as a toothbrush, and to be ready with a few hours' notice.

And all leave was cancelled.

CHAPTER 6

Nabbed

'We were, as one, completely and utterly gobsmacked. It was not unlike a horror story. It is still like a horror story. I'll say it again: we simply could not believe what was happening.'

Springtime in deepest Hampshire: what could be lovelier? Except that it was a particularly dark and misty May morning in 1955 that marked the departure of four leading telegraphist specialists L/Tel(S) from HMS *Mercury*. Although geared up and ready, we all felt somewhat apprehensive at the prospect of what would follow the familiar journey of twenty miles or so south to the ancient Royal Navy Dockyard at Portsmouth.

Her Majesty's Naval Base Portsmouth (HMNB Portsmouth) is one of three operating bases in the UK for the Royal Navy, the others being located at Clyde in Scotland and at Devonport which is about 175 miles west of Portsmouth on the same English Channel coast. Portsmouth is the headquarters for approximately 17,000 staff as well as a number of commercial shore interests with connections or an interest in the military. It's also, if you take a trip to the entrance of the old naval dockyard, home to a number of very popular tourist attractions, including HMS *Victory*, which was Lord Nelson's flagship (and is still a commissioned ship of the British Royal Navy, although it will never see the water again), and the restored remains of *Mary Rose*, the flagship of King Henry VIII.

The base at Portsmouth is the oldest in the Royal Navy and was, at one point, the largest industrial site of any kind in the world. Even today, it's an impressive sight when there are a few ships in the port and people invariably gather there and along the sea front to see one of the

Navy's bigger ships either leave for a spell in foreign waters or come home again. The whole place reeks of history and tradition; not that this was at the forefront of our minds that morning. History and tradition were all very well and nice, of course, for the visitors. But all we were concerned about was where we going and how long we'd be there for.

Even Percy, our transport driver and a one-time successful Royal Navy featherweight boxing champion, didn't have a clue as to our ultimate destination within the dockyard or the transportation we would be embarking in there – if, indeed, we even were. It remained a complete mystery. This was most unusual as Percy, along with the camp tailor, Split Waterman, was our eyes and ears and usually knew everything and anything that was going on. *Mercury*'s padre, John Scott, was also a good bet on knowing what was going on, but whether or not this was a divine blessing that had been bestowed upon him, He above only knows. Percy was always being called upon to transport our teams from place to place, probably because his personal motto was 'Hear all, see all and say bugger all', a quality that was well known even to inquisitive naval officers. Yet, on this occasion, even though he wouldn't have told us much anyway, it seemed as if even Percy was well and truly out of the loop: he did as he was told and that was it. In this instance, it had been to drive us to the semaphore tower in the Naval Dockyard where we had been instructed to wait. No further information was forthcoming.

Arriving at the main gate of Portsmouth dockyard, much to the astonishment of a sleepy MoD policeman, we were asked for our identity cards before even being allowed to continue, probably because no one was ever expected to arrive at that unearthly hour in the morning without some kind of prior arrangement. As we proceeded to journey the few hundred yards up to the semaphore tower building[1], Percy wished us well on our trip to 'wherever', leaving us bemused and wary as we took up a waiting position on the filthy and slimy steps beneath the tower. To add to the intrigue, we had been instructed to change our cap ribbons from HMS *Mercury* to plain HMS upon leaving our transport, something else that was very unusual.

---

1 The head office of the naval base commander and Queen's harbour master.

After standing on those cold granite steps for what seemed like half the day, we eventually became aware of a diesel engine approaching from the direction of the dockyard naval pond. As it got ever closer, this thumping and never-to-be-forgotten noise eventually drew our eyes to a well-weathered naval personnel vessel (MFV) slowly gliding to where we were standing, still and alert, like the statues on Easter Island. The MFV slowly, and amidst a cloud of sulphurous fumes, drew up alongside us, prompting its ageing skipper to shout for us to scramble aboard. As our feet left terra firma and before we even had the chance to reach the covered seats facing aft, the MFV was underway again with my immediate thought being how long it would be before I felt the earth of home beneath my feet again. We asked the skipper a few questions but all he would give us in response was, 'My orders are to proceed to the Nab Tower and wait.'

So that is what we did.

The Nab Tower is the welcome sight that sailors see when they are returning home from all four corners of the globe. Affectionately known as the 'Nab', this ancient fort is struck on the seabed at the eastern reaches of the Solent and the Isle of Wight. The Nab is one of three forts that were built in the Solent to warn of invasion by the French, and others, in days gone by and was later intended to serve as a lookout post for encroaching enemy submarines during the First World War. We were now heading out on a rising tide, shrouded in a mist that was drifting landwards from the south. We found ourselves making headway east at about five knots, quite alone in one of the busiest shipping crossroads in the world. The time now was 0330. Ashore, the lights of Southsea castle were gradually fading from view on our port stern with Bembridge, on the north-east coast of the Isle of Wight, just visible to starboard. Selsey Bill, jutting out into the Solent like a broken fingernail, was somewhere north on our port quarter. Those of you familiar with the weather forecast broadcast on Meridian local television will see, directly under the 'm' of Portsmouth, the hazardous moving sand and gravel banks upon which sea craft still manage to get stranded with monotonous regularity.

After half an hour or so, the MFV began to reduce speed, so that it was just about making headway against the turning tide. The rippling of the slightly choppy water on the MFV's clinker-built side was just about audible as we waited, nervously, for what was to come. Everything was still, even now, happening so slowly, but, just as had been the case in the preceding weeks, there was nothing we could do about it and the whole situation was starting to grind at our nerves. Then, quite suddenly, as we were staring out into the fading sea mist, we saw the silhouette of the infamous Nab Tower in all its glory. It's a visual welcome handshake to ships of all shapes and sizes and from nations too numerous to list, its appearance giving them reason to reduce their speed and, with it, prepare for the end of whatever journey they have made. As we had made our way out to the now ever more visible Nab, the most logical explanation that we could come up with between us was that a passing warship would be there to pick us up. This in itself wouldn't be particularly unusual though, so why the secrecy? There could only be one reason for that, a conclusion that was offered by an increasingly despondent Chalky: 'It's got to be something else.'

As we continued to wait, quite out of the blue, Taffy told us that he had been hoping to get engaged in a month's time in his home town on Barry Island in South Wales. None of us were particularly full of light and life at this moment in time but Taffy, in particular, was not a happy pixie. Nothing now made sense to him or any of us any more. Perhaps – another idea – we were going to be picked up by an Aquila Airways flying boat. The sea was calm enough and it was certainly something that had happened before. A few more suggestions followed but each one seemed to be even more outrageous than the former.

At one point, and, rather sheepishly, Taffy suggested we might be waiting for a submarine, a notion that was instantly discounted as none of us had ever been on a submarine and, even to be able to do so, one had to have attended and passed through that stringent submarine course that I had recently escaped having to do through joining the Radio Warfare branch.

That course was notorious and involved, amongst other things, having to go through the 100-foot salt water escape tower that is still prominent on the Gosport shoreline. The nearest any of us had been to this facility was either the wooden deck of the Gosport ferry or by being at the

Royal Naval Hospital at Haslar a couple of hundred yards due north up the road. So whatever it was we had been selected to do, at least joining the submarine service wasn't one of them.

I was at least, on this bleak morning, able to thank my lucky stars for that.

Stuck out in the Solent awaiting our fate I reflected that, although this wasn't a particularly favourable situation for me, it wasn't a frightening one either, not in the truest sense of the word. Unlike the time, for example, when I was stationed on the sweep deck of a minesweeper off Corfu, and a German mine which we had previously cut decided to float to the surface as we passed on a second run, having been drawn inwards against our starboard side by the ship's suction. Now that *was* frightening! The buffer, who was a very senior chief petty officer, actually shit himself as he tried to fend it off the side of our ship with a handy boat hook; 'I'm still here,' he shouted, in his usual jocular manner, grasping his crotch in a vain attempt to stop his bowel functions from reaching the deck. At that precise moment in time, it's fair to say that both he and the rest of us came mightily close to vying for jobs tending the flowers in St Peter's garden. And no, that CPO didn't get a gong or even a mention; such trifling deeds seldom did. If he'd have shovelled paper at the MoD for ever and a day as his backside spread over the years, he would have stood a far better chance of being rewarded for services rendered.

I was soon shaken back into the reality of the situation we were in by Chalky who suddenly cried out, 'What the hell are we doing, stuck out in the middle of the oggin, with half a bag of underwear, a few pairs of socks, a toothbrush, paste and little else, what the bloody hell is going on?' Chalky, a Royal Navy boxing champion, six-foot plus and built like a brick khazi,[2] was normally silent and quite tolerant of things. But now even he was uptight.

Then Taffy spoke. 'I've got it,' he said, 'I've got it. It's obvious, six weeks' worth of letter writing is a camouflage. Any one of us could have landed a cuddly buxom vivacious blonde millionaire nympho for a round-the-world cruise on an all-female-crewed luxury yacht, all expenses

---

2 An outdoor toilet.

paid. After all, we wouldn't need much underwear, that's for certain. Six weeks' worth of letters would easily have covered our getaway plus our next-of-kin forms for our loved ones, just in case we never returned.'

We found out later on that even our regulating Chief Wilkie hadn't had the slightest clue where we were going or into what situation. Much later, upon our return, he told us that our loved ones had been telephoning him and regularly asking the same questions, time after time and making him feel like a brainless imbecile, one whose own situation was being made all the worse by the letters that were piling up around him: letters that would remain unanswered.

Right now though, down by the Nab, something was, finally, happening.

Gradually, silently, becoming just about visible from behind the Nab Tower, a faint movement was observed, followed by a bewildering shape that was becoming more and more evident. My initial reaction was that I had to be seeing things, I just had to, and that the thing looming up ahead of us simply couldn't be there, it just couldn't.

Within moments, we were all gazing towards the faint silhouette of a submarine lying very low in the water and gradually moving towards us, almost invisible in the misty water. 'Probably on its way to *Dolphin*,' piped up Chalky, knowing full well, even as he uttered those words, that they had been spoken in faint hope rather than honesty. Never, in a million years, were we expecting a submarine. We'd laughed off Taffy's earlier suggestion that it might had been one and said, agreeing in unison, that, as none of us had been on the course at *Dolphin*, we couldn't go on a submarine, we were neither trained or qualified to do so. And yet, here, and getting ever close to us, was a submarine. A year or so previously, I had joined the Radio Warfare branch to avoid being sent into the submarine service yet here was one now, all ready to welcome me on board.

The MFV, with us as its human cargo, was quickly ordered alongside this long wet hunk of welded steel, one that was referred to by some, for good reason, as an 'iron coffin'. A voice then hailed us from the conning tower, telling us to throw over our bags before jumping onto the submarine's upper deck. Obviously that is what I did, along with the others, but I cannot, even now, remember jumping on board that submarine. All I can remember was the sight of one of our holdalls slowly slipping into the oggin before being expertly caught on a boat hook that was in the hands of an alert submariner. The four of us were now, like it or not, on board one of Her Majesty's submarines. We were, as one, completely and utterly gobsmacked. It was not unlike a horror story. It is still like a horror story. I'll say it again: we simply could not believe what was happening.

Suddenly, more instructions issued from the conning tower. We were now being told to drop our holdalls down the steep wet ladder forward and to follow on from there. Time was now of the essence. The submarine was alone and wished to stay that way. So, with holdalls clutched between our feet we stood, mesmerised, at the foot of the slippery iron ladder which we had just descended, squashed up together like a bunch of bananas and staring, in some amazement, at torpedo racks that were filled to the gunnels with bags, boxes, tins and sacks of all shapes and sizes. Anything, in fact, except for torpedoes. With hardly any room in which we could turn around, we remained in place, in shock, and staring into a maze, completely and utterly stunned. It goes without saying that none of us had ever been on a submarine before and, following those recent tragedies that had befallen the *Truculent* and *Affray*, no one amongst us in their right minds wanted to. For some peculiar reason, we had been declared immune from having to pass the stringent submarine course that included that hectic ascent of the 100-foot salt water escape tank. Now, as the forward escape hatch that we had just descended was hastily clipped shut, we felt a slight vibration under our feet which gave the impression that this huge chunk of steel was moving. By now, our sense of disbelief had been joined by another emotion, that of feeling completely overwhelmed. What was going to happen next?

I looked across at Taffy. Even he was standing stock still, his mouth agape as he took in the scene in complete astonishment. It was, at that precise moment, like something out of an Alfred Hitchcock film. For me, it still is. That sense of bewilderment and the tension that was steadily building around it was finally broken by, as if by magic, the arrival of the boat's coxswain. He was the senior lower-deck rating answerable to the captain and he now appeared from out of all the surrounding boxes and bags, telling us to follow him along the submarine's only gangway to the mess that we would be calling home for many weeks. So, by climbing over yet more boxes, tins, crates and bags, we eventually arrived in our new home, a mess for 35 men. The coxswain, who'd been regarding us as if we had just beamed down from outer space, managed to say, 'Stay here until we complete our trim dive. Leading Seaman Snow will be responsible for you until I return.'

Our arrival, both on the submarine and in that mess had, of course, taken everyone by surprise in the same way that it had us, and the looks we were now being given were only serving to make the situation feel even more traumatic. Eventually though, endeavouring to at least try to begin to understand what was going on, Taffy, very sheepishly, told the Leading Seaman that none of us had ever been on a submarine in our lives, not even during our Navy days spent at sea. Leading Seaman Snow quickly realised that we weren't joking and, amidst the alarm evident on all our faces and the stupid questions he was being bombarded with, he finally spoke, saying, with no little incredulity on his face, 'You mean to say you haven't been to *Dolphin* and up through the tank or done the submarine course?' His face was now ashen as he continued, 'I take it you don't know anything about escape or how to operate the DSEA escape gear or how to get through the airlocks for escape to the surface? It seems to me that you all know absolutely fuck all about submarines?'

'That just about sums it up,' quipped Taff. 'Fuck all.'

We later found out that on this and in any future operations, we couldn't have escaped anyway. It just wasn't an option. The four of us, now an integral part of a 68-man crew, were literally entombed. Before we'd arrived, the submarine's identity had been scrubbed off the conning tower and the closure of the forward hatch that the four of us had just descended had been followed by it being clipped and spot-welded shut, as was the escape hatch aft of the diesel room. The conning tower, on the other hand, had a double hatch system which wasn't welded shut; this was apparently in case we were rammed which was, of course, what had happened to the *Truculent* in the Thames estuary a few years previously.

Taffy, his usual Welshman's voice rather shaky, suddenly piped up, 'What's the name of this floating iron grocery store?' He was still a little bewildered, even a bit scared. '*Turpin*,' came the sheepish reply.

'I just can't believe it, how could they, the bastards…' Stopping in mid-sentence, Snowy was absolutely flabbergasted. I quickly reminded him, 'Ne… ne… neither can we believe it,' my childhood stutter coming to the fore for the first time since I don't know when.

By now a little calmer, Snowy went on to say that not only were we now a risk to ourselves, we were a risk to everyone on *Turpin* by not even knowing the basic rudiments of life on board a submarine. 'Your reasons for being on board had better be worth it', he mumbled, without the inevitable well-worn matelot's language whilst, as he said it and in the back of my mind, everything that had been happening to us over recent weeks began to make sense. Talk about being shoved in at the deep end.

'Hands secure from diving stations,' the tannoy very quietly rang out. We were under way proper. Diving stations encompasses both surfacing and diving.

HMS *Turpin* (www.maritimequest.com/Michael W. Pocock)

Snowy had now calmed down enough to tell us that this particular patrol had been planned for months. *Turpin* had completed some sea trials two days previously after a lengthy and very expensive refit in Chatham dockyard where, among other new operational requirements, it had been sliced in two before having an additional fourteen-foot hull section added. This was to accommodate extra electrical switchgear, an additional pair of updated electrical motors and associated batteries which allowed longer operational time as well as manoeuvrability when running deep, extra rib supports having been fitted to the welded pressure hull meaning that the 'safety depth' could now exceed 300 feet.

For the uninitiated, a submarine has to run on electrical motors when it is under periscope depth, hence the phrase 'running deep'. *Turpin*'s welded steel hull was streamlined which resulted in less drag; doing this had meant the removal of the four-inch gun and alterations to the conning tower that enclosed the periscopes and snorkel masts, something which gave the sub a more upright and smoother operational and cosmetic appearance. Both sonars, upper and lower, were updated with the very latest hoisting and lowering mechanism, similar in action to that which you see with the periscope.

The sub's radar, meanwhile, which, under normal circumstances, would have been in its own office as part of the control room, was landed ashore, together with its aerial. The batteries were also upgraded which meant *Turpin* had a faster submerged speed of up to about 12 knots, a capability that had to be meticulously regulated as this action drew huge amounts of current from those batteries. With the snort mast (a device that allows the submarine to take on air from above whilst operating under water) raised, which meant the sub could run on its diesel engines, its speed would, providing the weather was good, get up to about 20 knots. If the weather was bad, then, in order for the snort mast to be effective, it would have to be raised higher up above the water, something which would have increased *Turpin*'s radar fingerprint, a move seldom used as the consequences of doing so could put the submarine in extreme, if not suicidal danger.

From the submarine's name, we knew that *Turpin* was a 'T' (Triton) boat like, for example, HMS *Totem, Thule* and *Templar*; the tragically lost *Truculent* had also been one of the Royal Navy's 'T' boats. *Turpin*, along with a few others of this class that underwent a conversion, was re-classified as a 'Super T' boat, one that wasn't too dissimilar to the German Mk 21 U-boat (2000 series). Only a few of those were ever built and the end of the war meant that they never went to sea in hostile mode, something that the Allies, who were well aware of their offensive capabilities, were extremely relieved about. *Turpin* and *Totem* were amongst the Allies' response to these U-boats.

The outstanding question now within the boat was, especially given our arrival, 'Where are we going?' Snowy asked us the same question, expecting, I am sure, for us to have come aboard knowing just that. The look on his face when we told him our story, that we didn't even know we were being sent onto a submarine, never mind where we were going, absolutely beggars belief.

After a short time, the coxswain returned and issued us with some warm clothing in the shape of submarine white woollen sweaters called aprons. We then learnt that the 'old man' as the boat's captain is called, would make himself known as soon as we were safely outside the shipping lanes. The boat (a submarine is called a boat) was now to remain unseen at all times, running at a periscope depth of at least 33 feet under the surface. Spying eyes at this time would no doubt quickly put two and two together, observing a British submarine without a radar aerial and automatically wondering 'What's it up to?' Perhaps someone already was, for Southsea castle was a well-known location for prying eyes with its position at the entrance to Portsmouth's naval base, a well-known landmark where a spy might escape recognition as he or she stood mingling with the tourists, bent on watching Royal Navy ships leaving or entering the harbour on a daily basis, irrespective of the weather.

The strongest buzz doing the rounds on the boat as we made our way on a westerly course down the English Channel was that we were going into the Mediterranean then into either the Aegean or Adriatic Sea to land or pick up agents, something which had been undertaken several times previously. The obvious fly in the ointment with regard to that possibility, however, was the fact that not only had the boat's radar been removed, especially as it had never been deemed necessary for it to be taken out previously, but, and more tellingly, why this had coincided with four leading telegraphist specials being dropped aboard without anyone previously knowing that they were coming – including the specialists themselves! There were, of course, other buzzes. And these were much closer to home. One postulated that we were headed for the northern reaches of the Baltic, to St Petersburg or to the Finnish and Swedish sea areas which were seeing some troubled political times.

It was, to be fair, anyone's guess.

CHAPTER 7

Run Silent, Run Deep

'Where we're going, escape isn't an option. It's not on the agenda. At 10,000 feet, it's dark, bloody cold and pointless.'

Before *Turpin* had sailed, only the captain and maybe the navigating officer had known the sub's true destination, and, even then, it would have depended on whether the post-refit sea trials had been successful. Now, *Turpin*'s cruising speed of about ten knots, achieved by using the diesel engines, took us on a westerly course down the English Channel; but this soon altered as we changed course and headed towards the North Atlantic, having steered well clear of Fastnet Rock on the southern coast of Ireland. We soon realised that the boat had changed course as the steady momentum of sailing in the Channel gave way to a different 'feel', altering to a sideways movement that was in tune with the rolling turbulence of the often treacherous North Atlantic.

Our passage to the operational area, I now discovered, would take at least a further seven days. It would be during this time at sea that we would, very quickly, learn the ins and outs of how a submarine at sea operates when it is on a mission.

In general, half of the boat's crew would be on duty at any one time meaning, of course, that the other half would be off duty. This meant that our mess, which you can see in one of this book's photographs, had to find enough room for about 35 men. Which made it very crowded! So, although not everyone could get in at once, the fact that we had these shift patterns meant that it was never quite as bad as you first thought.

HMS *Turpin* – life in the mess (1955) (courtesy Tony Beasley)

A similar practice was applied to sleeping arrangements. Some of the crew slept in bunks, others in hammocks in the mess; others slept on more bunks that were in the main gangway that ran from the fore ends where the forward torpedoes were stowed, or would have been in normal circumstances. Bunks continued into and through the operations room and on into the diesel engine room.

Taff and I were allocated a bunk in the boat's only gangway which was known as the 'cabbage patch' as it was situated over the area where the fresh vegetables were stored. The bunk was the nearest to the ops room and not too far from the galley. Come harvest time, it was not unusual for the mattress to be sprouting carrots, onions, spuds and the like, all nice and fresh as we neared the end of a six-week or so trip, as Taff and I would find out. When the watch system was disturbed in any way, 'hot bunking' was the order of the day, meaning exactly what it says – one in, one out. If we ran deep for a rest, normally 120 feet down or so, or, through necessity, a lot deeper, whichever of the two of us was due to be on watch had to remain alongside our equipment in the radar room. This wasn't in case we were needed – our equipment couldn't be used if we were lower than periscope depth – it was because we had nowhere else to go. Besides, after a while, a swivel chair, with arms, is as good a place as any to nod off.

Occasionally, the 'old man' would allow 'one all round' meaning that those who smoked could have a quick cigarette, something that was only normally permitted to and from the operational areas. Surprisingly, very few people smoked, despite each man being allowed 300 duty-free cigarettes, known as 'blue liners' from their distinctive packing, per month. Cigarettes would be used when playing table games in lieu of coinage when betting was involved, as was rum and either sippers, gulpers or the whole tot which would have been neat pusser's rum. It was therefore not at all unusual at the end of any operation for thousands of cigarettes (or fag sticks as they were known) to either be ditched or kept by those who rolled their own. They were certainly in no condition to be smoked.

Books were in abundance, appearing in all of the nooks and crannies that could be found on board. Then there were all the usual board games, each of them played with the inevitable submarine variations: 'uckers (a traditional Navy board game not dissimilar to ludo), chess, backgammon, dominoes, chase the lady, bridge, canasta, pontoon, snap (usually at tot time), whist and rummy. I was surprised at how many in the mess would also spend hour after hour engaged in doing a crossword whilst one or two others were doing correspondence courses – a little difficult, given the circumstances. Games were played on a challenge league system which ended twice, once as we arrived and once as we departed station. One chess match in particular ended up becoming a quiet prelude to a rather eventful period in all of our lives.

One of the first experiences I encountered in the strange environment of the submarine was popping and irritation in both of my ears. This was something that I had to get used to over the first six weeks or so that I was aboard, although it has also affected me in the long term; ever since my days serving on *Turpin* I have suffered from tinnitus and hearing loss to varying degrees. Then there was the smell encountered when first descending *Turpin's* forward hatch, that rich potpourri of acid, diesel fumes, body odour, stinking feet, toilet smells, stale air and condensation, all mixed with the smell of food that was either on the turn or in the process of being cooked. It all took, I promise you, some getting used to. Even now, whenever my wife fills the car with diesel fuel, the slightest sniff of the stuff brings back memories. And it is always my wife who must fill the car; I do not have the strength to squeeze the nozzle at the pump due to the life-threatening injury sustained to my neck whilst I was on *Turpin*, one that affected both arms and hands.

Early on, we were taken on a tour of the operations room which is the nerve centre of the boat, the place where everything happens. Tucked away in an inglenook next to the now defunct radar office on the starboard (right) side was an area where all the chart work and verbal orders were recorded and all movements, bearings and sightings plotted. Now, I say 'all' the chart work; in reality, this was not necessarily the case as, occasionally, *Turpin* would stray into areas where we shouldn't have been. When that happened, I was to spend many an hour bent over those charts plotting 'S' band radars ashore and taking bearings of other shore-based 'X' band radar intercepts, which were mobile.

Turpin's ELINT equipment (at least there was something on board we were familiar with) had been fitted by two of our own senior branch chief petty officers. It occupied the radar compartment which opened out into the operations (ops) room. The aerials for this equipment were placed on top of the snort mast and aft periscope mast with leads running from the base of these masts trailing some eight feet or so over the deck into the ELINT equipment situated in the now radar-less office. The slack of these ELINT leads was vulnerable to being caught and would often snap when the snort periscopes were raised and lowered, especially during crash diving.

Thus the ELINT equipment became the eyes of the submarine in place of the radar. Taffy, although a Russian linguist, was now my very able assistant and relief, with the radar office now my mess and its swivel chair my bed for many an hour. In truth, it became quite comfortable after a few days, knowing that one had little choice when working but to 'sit, concentrate, watch and wait'.

The ELINT equipment could only come into operational mode when the boat was at periscope depth, which is 33 feet below the surface. At this depth, the periscopes and snort mast, which carried the ELINT aerials for our equipment, are hoisted about three feet or so above the water (the final height depends on the sea state at the time) to scan the horizon and sky.

To the uninitiated, the snort mast, a Dutch invention towards the end of the Second World War, is a device which, when raised above the water, sucks in the air essential to operate the diesel engines which propel the boat as well as keeping the boat's huge banks of batteries charged. Diesel engines have two requirements to work, air and fuel, and their reliability is essential as the battery power they provide is of paramount importance. Without any battery power, a boat is completely useless. At times, when the battery output was very low and, more often than not in the operational area, the amount of air reaching the crew was limited, over time that started to become quite noticeable as the environment we were working in started to become a little bit stale and malodorous. This was, of course, a completely new experience for the likes of me, Taffy and the others but was also new to the existing crew who had never been in such a situation before. 'A breath of fresh air' is a cliché that is often heard in jest of course, yet, within the confines of a submarine, it can be a life saver. Conversely, it is little use having plenty of battery power when the boat is lying deep if the crew are as listless as they tend to be after a good run ashore.

The question of 'fresh air' came to the attention of the outside world the day before the Second World War broke out in 1939 when another 'T' boat, *Thetis*, became firmly stuck, bows down, in the mud at the bottom of Liverpool Bay. It had been undergoing initial sea trials and had some 100 men aboard when something went disastrously wrong. With the stern fully out of the water by some nineteen feet, men could be heard hammering on the submarine's side. At this point, a hole could, quite easily, have been cut out of the visible part of the submarine to allow the men to escape to safety, but this option was not taken. Four members of the ship's company were able to use the escape chamber to safely exit the vessel, but the fifth crew member panicked and opened the outer hatch too early, resulting not only in his own death by drowning but also rendering the hatch inoperable. The remainder of the crew ultimately died an agonising death through lack of breathable air. The book *The Admiralty Regrets* by co-authors C.E.T Warren and James Benson tells this story remarkably well if you wish to find out more.

The difference that clean air makes to a boat's crew who have been breathing in a submarine's foul and noxious recycled air is quite noticeable. Under normal conditions, submariners may not have had to deal with this; however, the conditions we were operating under were anything but normal. The crew had never before experienced being short of air to breathe and, as we later found out, they had never experienced being continuously submerged for weeks on end either. So, despite my and my mates' complete inexperience when it came to submarines at that time we were all, at least, in the same boat when it came to this. During the Second World War, German U-boats were often forced to surface for want of air – they didn't have the choice, it was a case of either they surfaced or the entire crew suffocated.

Our risk of being detected if we surfaced, whether that be for taking on clean air or not, depended on the height above the water of the snort and periscope masts, necessarily clear of the water as they carry the ELINT and SIGINT aerials. This made our radar fingerprint much larger which meant we could be detected at a noticeably more distant range, say horizontal level ten to twelve miles. Generally, the larger the ship, the higher the transmitting aerial has to be, meaning the distance at which signals may be received is much greater than those from, for example, a low-lying Russian Kotlin-class destroyer. The lower an 'X' band radar transmitting aerial is, however, the greater the chance it has of detecting a periscope as the lobe, the area of the radar transmission, is much nearer the water. I ended up writing a paper proposing that surface ships have an 'X' band receiving aerial fitted onto their bows for this reason. Transmissions from aircraft, on the other hand, using the lower frequency 'S' band, have a greater range but what is gained in operating from a great height and distance is lost considerably in definition.

Back to day-to-day life on the submarine now and the question of drinking water. This was, not surprisingly, in very short supply and what little was available tasted absolutely terrible, although I maybe shouldn't even use the word 'terrible' as it was actually tasteless. Washing was, at best, a damp flannel wrapped around one's chops and, with luck, sometimes other areas. Cleaning teeth was virtually water free and 'as it should be' according to my daughter, who is an orthodontist – not that we had a choice! Conserving water is a matter of self-discipline instilled in all submariners. You don't waste water.

Everything is controlled from the operations room, from diving and surfacing to 'blowing the heads' – that is, giving the toilets a good old clean out. These too were crammed with provisions, so much so, that there was hardly enough room to wipe one's bum. There were no toilet doors either as they took up too much space. All movement throughout the boat had to be authorised by the control room – and that even included walking. Too much movement from one area to another would upset the trim of the boat which could have been, and indeed has been in the past, quite disastrous for both the submarine and the entire crew. With the extra provisions now on board, the 'trim dive' (a manoeuvre to re-establish the neutral buoyancy point of a submersible craft, a procedure that the German U-boats performed on a daily basis) took some time. Provisions such as fuel and water have to be evenly distributed throughout the submarine to make it seaworthy. A close watch on fuel levels was crucial at all times, with this responsibility lying with the engineer officer, although the overall responsibility of 'trimming the boat' is the responsibility of the first lieutenant who is also the second-in-command. The trim dive is truly a mammoth task and would need to be done many times.

Our daily tot was issued with the 'big' meal of the day which could be at any time, depending on the activities taking place on the boat at the time. This meant that sometimes we'd have a main meal twice within a 24-hour period whilst, on other occasions, it didn't occur for many an hour or even days. Often, if you were staring at a ship's clock, you had no idea if it was morning or evening unless a 24-hour timepiece was to hand and, as far as the day of the week was concerned, that would often be nothing more than a guess. However, when we did eat, no matter what the time of day it was, I have to say that the food on *Turpin* was the best I have tasted on any ship that I have served upon – and there are more than I care to remember. Now cooking food in such a small and compact environment does, of course, have its drawbacks, mainly that of smell. The smell of cooking and the food does, in time, combine itself with all the other smells on the boat and they all linger for so long that, after a while, you really cannot differentiate one smell from another. The worst smell is, without a doubt, that which is given off by the acid from the batteries, especially during a long charge after being forced to go deep and play cat and mouse with any hostile destroyers above that are constantly 'pinging' you before lobbing a few depth charges your way.

Talking of bad smells, we once carried a lot of tinned turkey on board. One such tin had apparently blown open prior to its being opened, meaning that the boat smelt of rotten turkey for days; a change, I suppose, from the usual mix of diesel fuel and acid fumes. Even the 'old man' couldn't stand that smell of bad turkey and, at the first opportunity, he made sure we dragged in some fresh air; it helped, of course, but the smell did still linger on for a few days afterwards.

The ship's galley, where all the food-related activity took place, was less than twenty feet square. Apart from having to cook meals for 68 men, the cook also made bread and umpteen rolls daily whenever circumstances permitted it. When ship's activities livened up, then ship's biscuits or hard tack were the order of the day. After the sort of skirmish which might have had us chewing on a hard old bit of biscuit for a while, the 'old man' would often take the boat down to about 120 feet so we could enjoy a bit of peace, have a slap-up meal and enjoy a well-earned tot. If electrical power was a bit 'iffy' however, the cook wouldn't always be able to serve us that big meal.

We were all learning therefore that, despite any privations that we might have to temporarily go through in the process, conserving battery power was, as much as possible, something that had to be done at all times, a situation that, up until our arrival on board, the *Turpin* crew had never really been in before. We were, in that matter, all learning and coping with that aspect of submarine life at the same time. When the periscope was up, the 'old man' always had his arms wrapped around its handles, making an all-round 360-degree sweep of both the seas around us and the sky, his eyes almost permanently affixed to the viewer. Occasionally, if a call of nature dictated that he temporarily disengage himself from the periscope, he'd allow the navigating officer the opportunity to take a look for a couple of minutes or so. Sod's law being what it is, of course, such a departure from the norm dictates that 'happenings' will tend to occur at exactly those times.

One thing in submarines' favour compared with surface ships was that diesel electric boats ran a lot quieter than they ever could, something which suited me fine. I also now understand that boats like the *Turpin* were much quieter than the modern nuclear submarines are and that, because they were quieter, would be a lot more difficult to detect than their modern-day counterparts. This is a fact that both the Russian and American navies have realised in recent years, so much so that they are both, once again, building diesel electric submarines.

The camaraderie on submarines is amongst the highest order and by far the most noticeable I have experienced in the whole of my 24 years and over 30 ships serving in the Royal Navy. Submariners may be branded crabby and happy but, take it from me, they have to be – and are. In addition to that observation, I was also taken aback by the closeness of the officers to the crew on *Turpin*, something that was very apparent from my first day on board. The boat's captain (the 'old man') was a senior lieutenant commander who, in the control room, was, of course, referred to as 'Sir', and this was prim, proper and correct. Many of the crew on *Turpin* were addressed by both officers and crew by their first name, or the name they acquired by virtue of their job or where they came from, or, in some occasions, their mannerisms. Thus names like 'Lofty', 'Jock', 'Brummie' or 'Ginge' prevailed; likewise 'Sparks', 'Chef', 'Planes' or 'Pings'. This familiarity would be completely foreign to life on a surface ship where the captain is generally a loner whilst the other officers tend to avoid getting too close to the crew.

It's not snobbery though, it's just the way they are following their training in Dartmouth and the obligatory 'knife and spoon' course that follows in Greenwich where they are taught, amongst other things, how to talk properly and to maintain a superior deportment, irrespective of whether they know what they are talking about or not. Officers are always 'right', even if it is proven otherwise – for example, in dialogue with a chief petty officer (a non-commissioned officer, in other words, a man who was worked his way up the ladder) whose naval experience could best be proved by the rows of medals he had glued to his chest.

This sort of friction had been behind Taffy's outburst when, up on a charge, he'd invited the young divisional officer who barely knew him to take the proverbial run and jump off the ship's side before adding, 'I've got three kids older than you'. Taff was, of course, cautioned for his misconduct but, afterwards, the ship's captain was seen to be having a word in the divisional officer's ear, effectively saying to him, 'Perhaps you should learn and listen a bit more'. Hardly a reprimand but, nonetheless, in saying what he did, the captain was still noting Taff's long service and experience and suggesting that young officers might benefit by making the most of that sort of knowledge. I should add though, admirable as this was, I seldom, if ever, heard a naval officer acknowledge a non-commissioned man with a 'please', 'sorry' or even a 'thank you'. Mind you, my own belief that the men 'below decks' rather than the officers are the ones that the Royal Navy couldn't do without was confirmed by someone of an extremely high rank when I had the chance to spend some time in his company in 1974. That man was Lord Louis Mountbatten, a former First Sea Lord, Chief of the Defence Staff and Admiral of the Fleet from

1956 through to 1960. He'd joined us in the senior rates' mess at HMS *Mercury* at the annual meeting of the Royal Navy Chief Communicators Association, of which he was the president. We were all in the middle of a discussion when Lord Louis made it abundantly clear that the Royal Navy was run by his chief petty officers and petty officers, following this up by saying a ship could operate without officers but it could not operate without chief petty officers and petty officers!

How very true.

As a footnote to that little theme, it has to be said that, as we progress ever further into the digital age where many on the lower decks are actually better qualified than their superiors, it is inevitable that this barrier between the officers and ratings will and must take a gradual turn towards a mutual understanding and respect that will make for better efficiency throughout a ship.

***

Following the boat's altering of course from the relatively calm waters of the English Channel, the dual tides began to move us about much more, especially as we left the south-west coast of Ireland. We were now well away from the busier shipping lanes, steadied on a northerly course as *Turpin* ploughed onwards through the deeper, colder and more turbulent waters of the North Atlantic. One hazard that did have to be negotiated was one that also operated well clear of the shipping lanes – that of fishing trawlers. To put it bluntly, the trawlers were a bloody nightmare, seemingly able to creep up on you at will as they towed their deep-sea nets that were often many miles long. *Turpin*, being unseen, had to take emergency avoiding action on more than one occasion; doing this on our run north, when we were topped up with liquids and food, was a far from easy task.

Aware of our new course as I leaned over the chart, I hazarded a guess that we were steering for the Barents Sea, the domain of the Russian Navy's Northern Fleet, rather than heading into the relatively safe waters of the Baltic. Whatever our destination, we had to take the Atlantic route and, once our navigating officer changed our charts by unrolling a cleaner (unused) and larger one, this could only mean one thing: we were indeed off to the infamous Barents Sea, home of the formidable Soviet fleet.

The Barents Sea was not completely unfamiliar territory to me. I didn't have to look back too far to recall my days on HMS *Truelove* and others playing dodgems in that stretch of water with the suicidal Icelandic trawlers that also headed out there. This time we were below the waves and, now that we had confirmation of where we were going, Taffy looked over at me and shrugged his shoulders as he glared at the new chart, one that we would now be constantly referring to in the operational area. Years later, I could still draw that chart in detail, including where the shore-based 'S' band sites and carefully disguised 'X' band radar installations were, one of which, in a particular area within Kola (a peninsula in the far north-west of Russia) appeared to be a mobile station. Another area within Kola and the neighbouring Rybachi peninsula was enclosed in red and noted, 'Minefield: precise area unknown', the sort of statement that was apt to bring a little colour to your cheeks.

The area we were due to patrol was the exercise area of the surface ships and submarines based around the Kola Inlet and Rybachi, downriver from the Russian City of Murmansk, with our ultimate destination to be deep inside the Arctic Circle. The submarine fleet there alone consisted of over thirty operational boats and, although GCHQ had previously given us a hint as to what exactly the Russian fleet up there comprised, much of the information supplied was speculation, innuendo and dodgy intelligence, especially any information that was supplied by our allies as that most certainly could not be relied upon.

In the mid-1950s, ten years after the Second World War had finished, *Turpin* and *Totem* were the very first British diesel electric submarines to be specially adapted to undertake this very dangerous work. No other boats had come anywhere close to this region to engage in the activities that we were now committed to carrying out, so we were very much the pioneers of Barents Sea espionage of this nature. At least all the classroom hours that I had put in, with Taffy and the others, over the years would now come in handy, as well as having to roll our guts out on the fishery protection minesweepers whilst playing hide and seek with the Icelandic Navy during the Cod Wars. All of that work, which now seemed very much a means to this end, had certainly given us a hint of what to expect around Nordkapp in Norway and eastwards, deep into the Barents Sea and Kola.

As we crept further north, fishing trawlers were once again becoming a very real hazard. They seemed, as was their wont, to suddenly appear from nowhere so the sonar specialists' main work was now a steady two-man operation maintaining their positions. This remained the case until we left the vicinity of the Shetland Islands where trawler activity became more manageable. The 'old man' was particularly wary of the trawls (nets) which, as I have already said, could be many miles long. Without radar, these were now much more of a threat to us than had we been navigating the English Channel.

Once, quite out of the blue, I had occasion to ask the coxswain about how we might escape *Turpin* if we needed to do so. His reply, which sometimes comes back to me to this day in nightmares, was, 'Escape? Where we're going, son, escape isn't an option. It's not on the agenda. At 10,000 feet, it's dark, bloody cold and pointless.'

Not long after this particularly enlightening piece of dialogue, I had managed to squeeze myself into the mess for a couple of hot bread rolls and my tot when, being nearest to the gangway, I was asked to fetch a tin of Kye (a form of drinking chocolate) from one of the escape apparatus lockers. These were used to stow equipment for use of escape through the boat's hatches up into the open sea. These lockers were spread throughout the boat which meant we had around 30 per cent more lockers than crew. Finding a row of these metal lockers near to the 'cabbage patch' where I slept, I found they were either full of tinned food and packets or spot-welded shut. In other words, all escape apparatus had been removed. This brought back to my ears the words of the coxswain and exactly what he meant by 'pointless'. All of our escape gear had followed the same route as our radar and *Turpin's* four-inch gun – it had all well and truly gone.

It isn't just in the movies where the square-jawed heroes are told they are heading out on a 'suicide mission' and accept it in their usual stoical manner. We also had to accept it.

I now began to realise why the crew were asked if they were married and were given the option of staying ashore if they were. And, in fairness to our leaders, after spending hundreds of thousands of pounds of tax payers' money refitting *Turpin* and *Totem* with the very latest modifications to carry out these extremely dangerous covert operations that were so very badly needed at the time, a handful of twenty-odd-year-old specialists plus the crew and boat would all be seen as well worth any sacrifice that might have to be made. We were all part of the unofficial action that took place throughout the Cold War and operating under the 'need to know' basis. In short, we all knew what we were letting ourselves in for.

Today I completely understand this, yet, at the time, I never gave it a thought. Even so, sixty years later, I do wonder what downright lies the Admiralty would have dreamt up to pacify our loved ones if anything had happened to us. The prospect of such a disaster was no fantasy. Our escape gear would have helped had we been in a situation similar to that of the submarine *Truculent*, rammed in relatively shallow water at the mouth of the Thames; it would also have been helpful if we'd needed to leave the boat in the English Channel or even immediately off Kola. However, with the benefit of hindsight, the submarine and all its crew were all expendable and, given the tinderbox situation the world was in at that time, I now agree with the MoD's prevailing logic back then.

Prior to every covert operation carried out, the permission of the Prime Minister had to be obtained before these patrols departed. Such clandestine operations at the very height of the Cold War had to take place as the information they could have garnished for NATO forces was priceless. So, for such operations, the majority of the boats' crews were in their early- to mid-twenties except for the few chief petty officers, petty officers and a couple more officers we had on board with us.

At that age, we really did anything that was asked of us although, in reality, we had little choice but to do so. The general public, I have to say, were probably not quite so gullible as to believe what they were told and, had we been lost, I am sure that the 'official' explanation would have been met with scepticism by some. But then there is always a mixture of lies, cover-ups and mystery whenever any ship is lost at sea, especially with submarines, for the simple fact that no-one usually witnesses the loss unless they have a vested interest in it. Which means that pretty much anything can be offered up as the reason for the loss of a submarine whilst it is on active service.

One such case, of many, occurred in February 1968 when the American submarine *Scorpion* was en route back to its US base after a stopover in Rota, off the coast of Spain. Crew letters at the time indicate that *Scorpion* might not have been a particularly happy ship. It had suffered from numerous mechanical breakdowns as well as an electrical fire that broke out near the waste disposal unit.

Despite the fact that these written accounts from the crew seem to indicate that *Scorpion* was not fit for active service, it eventually departed Riga under orders to seek out any Soviet ships that might have been in the vicinity of the Azores at that time before returning to its home port in the United States. All must have seemed fairly routine until, towards the end of May 1968, *Scorpion's* captain transmitted the news that they had located a Soviet submarine at a depth of 110 metres (around 360 feet) and that he was, as per their orders, about to commence surveillance of that craft.

Still all seems routine, doesn't it? Cold War cat and mouse. Except that this was the last message that anyone received from *Scorpion*.

A search commenced the following month, one that was, fortunately, able to be narrowed down to a specific area as a naval listening station on the Canary Islands had captured fifteen 'acoustic events' (which basically means explosions) that had taken place off the Azores in a period of time that had lasted just over three minutes.

There was now little to no doubt in anyone's mind, at least unofficially, that *Scorpion* had been lost, and with all hands.

The submarine was later found 3,000 metres (its maximum operating depth had been a little over 200 metres) down at the bottom of the ocean. *Scorpion* had gouged a vast trench across the ocean floor at the denouement of its loss and the conning tower had been torn off, such was the force of the explosions that had sunk and destroyed it.

Numerous theories abounded as to what might have happened. Perhaps someone, somewhere, knows exactly how this sub met its fate. One theory postulated that it had accidentally fired one of its own torpedoes which, having no obvious target to aim for, had rounded back onto the vessel that had launched it in the first place. Another theory suggests that the aforementioned waste disposal unit may have led to the boat's demise after a failed valve allowed the ingress of sea water. The reaction between the salt water and *Scorpion*'s batteries would have produced hydrogen gas which, ultimately, ignited, leading to the explosions. A variant on this theme claimed that it was indeed a hydrogen explosion that had caused the disaster after excessive energy being sent to the batteries released a build-up of the gas, with the same fatal end consequences.

But perhaps the most chilling theory of all was that *Scorpion* had been sunk by either a Soviet submarine or a torpedo launched from one of their helicopters. Some people believed that this was a 'revenge' attack in response to the loss of the Soviet submarine *K-129* a couple of months earlier, sent to the bottom, it was claimed, after being rammed by the US submarine that was following it. Not totally impossible to believe. It's not as if there was no history of such an event happening. Remember that incident between the USS *James Madison* and the Soviet submarine off the Scottish coast in 1974? There had been precedents so little wonder that it might, intentionally or not, have happened again.

Not only was life aboard a submarine potentially extremely dangerous – even when you were going about your everyday business – it was also, as I was learning, a part of military service where, it seemed, crew and ship alike were seen almost as being expendable if the risk being taken was worth it. Not so much 'death or glory', more 'this never happened or glory'. In other words, we did as we were expected to do or we became a minor footnote and were forgotten about. I was soon to find out that this was exactly how we and our missions were considered by some.

When the four of us heard how the rest of the submarine's crew had been given tests and options before *Turpin* sailed, and actually been asked whether they wanted to take part in the top-secret operation we seemed to be on, expletives in both English and Welsh could be clearly heard as well as the inevitable questions about the parentage of various matelots on board. But how could we be anything other than aggrieved at the situation that we now found ourselves in? We were considered expendable. When I look back at that mission today, it seems completely unbelievable that we were literally shanghaied onto *Turpin* off the Nab whilst the powers that be, safe in their cosy offices, knew full well our chances of returning home were less than evens. The way in which I have been treated by the MoD since I sustained the injury I got whilst serving aboard the *Turpin* makes me think their attitude is no different today: we are all still expendable to them. To top it all, the mandarins in the MoD have the audacity to throw the Official Secrets Act your way if you attempt to speak in protest about how you were treated.

The secrecy surrounding our mission almost had another unwelcome consequence for us. Submariners earn their submarine pay and what is known as a 'hard layers allowance', a payment that is granted in return for sleeping rough – which you most certainly do on a submarine. Initially, however, both I and the team who had also joined *Turpin* on that chilly Sunday morning were not granted either of these allowances. The reason for that decision was that someone on HMS *Mercury*'s pay

HMS *Turpin* (courtesy www.maritimequest.com/Michael W. Pocock)

section might have connected those payments with the fact that we were now serving on a submarine, the knowledge of which might well have ended up compromising our work and the whole operation – we weren't, if you remember, 'on' *Turpin* at all, not officially. Eventually, and long after our covert operations on *Turpin* had been completed, the sub-lieutenant paymaster himself was 'persuaded' to credit our pay ledgers with what we had earned, something I am sure they would not have done so voluntarily. These lucrative tax-free payments amounted to ten shillings submarine pay and three shillings and sixpence hard layers per day, something that was eventually paid thanks to the efforts of our boss, Lieutenant Commander 'Chips' Selby Bennett SB ('SB' was the co-ordination control between covert submarine operations and GCHQ) who seemed to have mystical powers of persuasion with regard to anything that he did – fortunately for us.

***

Turpin was now on a steady northerly course and responding well to the different and often aggressive sea state that we were sailing in, albeit 33 feet below the waves, which is where we were to remain for the coming six to eight weeks. This was a far cry from what had been increasingly monotonous weekly exercises which involved playing war games, something we all hoped would never become a reality. Little did any of us suspect just how close we were, at the time, to World War Three until we were thrust into the top-secret world of covert operations. Up until then, most of those submariners didn't have the slightest idea what the Cold War was about, that's if they had even heard of the Cold War and what its possible implications might have been.

Steering well clear of the shipping lanes and avoiding deep-sea trawlers, we passed the Faroe Islands, leaving them well in the distance on our port side, and continued our northerly passage into the hazardous deep waters of the North Atlantic and, beyond those, the treacherous cold and icy Barents Sea. This is a vast graveyard of many goods-laden Allied ships as well as the thousands of gallant Royal and Merchant Navy men who lost their lives in the attempt to bring much-needed food and equipment to northern Russia in the Second World War – that same Russia which, as part of the USSR, was now a mistrusted enemy nation that would have willingly waged war on Britain and its former wartime allies given the slightest of provocation to do so. Little did we know just how close we were all sailing towards that very thing taking place.[1]

Thought provoking indeed.

The reason for our covert trip into hostile waters had been down to a report that had been given by a boffin at GCHQ. They had received some intelligence that the Russian navy, whose waters we were fast approaching, were being equipped with a new type of short-range radar, the characteristics of which little was known, except that it operated on a frequency higher than 'X' band which they, temporarily at least, were calling 'Q' band. It was believed to be a beamed type radar that was similar to existing gunnery radars. *Turpin* had been invited to sail into hostile Russian waters in order to find out more about this perceived new frequency and to listen to and record it in operation so that the aforementioned boffins could get to work on understanding it more. The report writer had mentioned, 'tongue in cheek' as he put it, that if we were to come across this, for now, 'phantom' radar, the likelihood was that the transmitting source would be very close indeed, that is, at most, just two and a half to three miles away. No one was in any doubt as to how potentially dangerous our mission was if it meant we were expected to get as close as that, and closer, to Russian ships whilst, in doing so, remaining completely invisible to them.

In general, our 2,000-mile trip to the exercise areas of the Barents Sea that were used by the ships and submarines of the Russian Northern Fleet was much the same as any other. We'd maintained, running on our diesel engines, an average speed of 10 knots whilst sailing 33 feet beneath the surface before, after around six or seven days, reaching the western fringes off Kirknes, the border town that lay between friendly Norway and hostile Russia.

With our batteries fully charged, fairly fresh air filling our lungs and tot time passed, the crew began to settle down to a very welcome nutritious

---

1 For further information, see the book *S.O.E* by historian M.R.D. Foot in which he writes, '...without Russian help, Great Britain would have lost the war against Germany'.

meal. Cooking in a galley of about only 20 square feet was a true art; nevertheless, our chef was more than adept in turning out a welcome hot meal to feed 68 hungry submariners. On most days he would also bake bread and buns, circumstances and electrical power permitting. The food, as I have already written, was amongst the best that I have ever tasted in any ship or shore establishment with the only real problems occurring when the ingredients needed ran out. At such times I would subsist on the carrots that could be harvested from the cabbage patch that was sprouting from beneath my bunk.

As we ate, we knew that the last remaining fishing trawlers that we had been detecting as we sailed ever further northward were now fading away out to the west, meaning that our radio operators were now able to concentrate on much larger fish: that is, Russia's mighty Northern Fleet that was based in and around Murmansk. This was the northernmost city of the Soviet Union, a port into which, less than ten years earlier, Allied merchant ships had sailed, welcome providers of food and supplies for their war effort. We were now running quiet on battery power which the diesel engines had been charging for most of our northern journey. The pervading smell of acid during and after a long charge is close to intolerable, worse than anything else I can think of. It just hangs about in the air for ages in the same way smoke does from a bonfire.

During previous operations, ELINT activity from Russian naval sources prior to entering our patrol area had, we'd been advised, been particularly abundant. However, on this particular occasion, HE was only detecting noise emanating from whales and fish whilst, in tandem with the lack of HE reception, my ELINT reception also became non-existent. Silent routine was now ordered throughout the boat; it could be that the Russians knew we were there and were playing a waiting game, as had certainly been the case on previous occasions. However, the longer this situation persisted, the tension that was showing amongst the crew steadily began to grow. There seemed no reason why I shouldn't be picking up ELINT signals; we were running at periscope depth which meant that my aerials were still operational. In addition to that, the weather up top was fair and periscope visibility was generally good. The silence was even beginning to have an effect on the 'old man' whose arms would embrace the periscope in an ever tighter fashion as it travelled round and round, up and down without a break, sight, sign or sound of any kind. To make matters worse, we had entered a period of light slushy and blustery rain, so it was looking as bleak above the water's surface as it was feeling beneath it. The captain looked completely worn out and, by now, it was clear to me that inviting our ELINT equipment to do something, to do anything, was only serving to make our presence felt and was not only becoming tedious, given the results we were (not) getting, but dangerous as well. Clearly, all was not well.

Each time the periscope dropped, I had to ensure that my leads were clear of the well that it dropped into, in case they ended up being snapped off – about all the action I was seeing at this time. All I could do, all we could all do, was to play a waiting game, to be patient and to just continue to listen; not, to be fair, that uncommon a practice for me and I was, by now, used to it. Known as a person who makes instant decisions, I also possess the asset of being patient, sometimes to my detriment. Described by some as being a 'loner', I suppose that, if I was, then most of us in our small naval branch could equally well be seen that way. It didn't particularly bother me; why run with the pack anyway? Loner or not, I wonder if I was the only person on board *Turpin* at that time who was nursing a sixth sense that something was about to happen just as the order 'No movement through the boat' was whispered from man to man as we settled down to wait and listen some more, the silence punctuated only by a pencil falling and hitting the deck, the noise it made in doing so echoing around the tense control room like a ton of dislodged bricks.

As I wrote above, the advent of that slushy rain and an increasing wind on the surface meant that periscope use was now becoming unreliable. With my ELINT telling us next to nothing and the HE still only managing to report sea-related noises, the 'old man', whose knuckles were glowing a pearly white, such was the tight grip he had on the periscope, bent over towards me to ask if I was confident that my equipment was working? My answer, and I had no reason to say otherwise, was 'Yes Sir'. Then, looking across the room, he asked the same question of the HE operator who gave a similar response although, by this time, the ice, fish and whale noise was now much less apparent than had been normal.

He might have been reassured that all was well with the boat's electronic eavesdropping equipment but, even so, the 'old man' was still less than happy. Neither, come to that, were we, stood around, all silent, all motionless (at such times, if the call of nature made itself known, you either had to hold it in or let it all out where you stood!). We were all on tenterhooks with only the, now almost silent, HE and ELINT systems the only means of establishing the safety of the boat. The visibility up top, which had been steadily deteriorating, was now getting worse which meant that the already tense situation on board was becoming even worse. As for what I'd said, even though I had reassured the 'old man' that all was well, I was now beginning to wonder if my equipment really was working properly; the seeds of doubt had now been planted in my mind.

The weather was, by now, continuing to run on a force three or four against a six-knot tide east to west. We were making about six knots running on batteries only and against the tide so, in effect, we were almost stationary. The tension continued to grow with silent routine in force throughout the boat whilst the no movement order also remained in place. It was like walking on frog spawn with the only thing we were really able to do if our eyes met across the control room was shrug our shoulders and express then way we felt in the look or body language we offered in return whilst, all the time, trying to keep the boat on an even keel against a turbulent tidal flow and pockets of extremely cold water.

After what seemed to be an age, the 'old man' whispered for the watches to be changed, one man at a time. Watching him from my position that was only a few feet distant, I found I could almost read his mind and the way he was thinking as he quietly made his requests. This must have been a unique situation for him as it certainly was for us. The only vaguely reassuring note was that the HE was continuing to pick up whales and fish, although it still wasn't doing so very often and certainly not as frequently as you might have expected it to. As for my ELINT equipment, whether that was working correctly or not was sheer guess work. I certainly had no reason to believe that it wasn't; the only problem was that I also had no reason to believe that it was.

My ELINT aerials, perched on top of our periscope and snort mast, now had to be raised a little in order to compensate for the worsening sea state above us. It was now running at a force four to five with the strong tide also beginning to throw us about more than usual, a sign that some really bad weather was about to break. All sorts of scenarios were now beginning to enter the equation as far as I was concerned, as I began to imagine a series of 'what ifs', 'perhapses' and all the other ifs and buts that seep their way into one's mind in similar circumstances. That's assuming, of course, there were any similar circumstances to the one that we were now in. But, try as I might to think of them, one didn't come to mind.

Today, over sixty years on, I still have nightmares about those dark hours. Writing about it doesn't help.

The situation we were in was a most unusual one. The usual dummy traffic was flowing freely, suggesting that nothing untoward was going on, at least nothing that the Admiralty had any knowledge about. The normal Russian submarine broadcasts, straight from the Ural mountains on 23 kcs, were being received without too many problems whilst we were also able to read the submarine broadcasts that was coming in from Rugby at 16 kcs. If something, somewhere, had have been flagged up as a cause of concern, then our signal units, known as 'Y' stations, which we had throughout the world, would have picked up the traffic and passed it onto GCHQ at Cheltenham. They would then have made their concerns about whatever it was clear to the Admiralty in London from where it would, ultimately, have been made to us. But nothing significant was happening and, as we maintained our silent stance, the only immediate problems that the 'old man' had to contend with were those of a rather more intimate nature, these being the ever more desperate requests from men to use the boat's heads.

As for myself, having relieved Taff on watch, I was surprised to see him return and even more surprised that the message he passed on wasn't related to the current situation we were in, not, at least, with regard to our running silent and wondering just what the hell was going on up there. No, Taff had heard from the 'old man' who had said, providing I agreed, that in order to help dispel some of the tension that was building around the ship, all of the ship's internal play-off matches, including the chess match that was due to be played between myself and the first lieutenant, were now to be played. We did and it went to three legs. Let's just say I came second and leave it at that.

With the chess matches taking up a fair bit of time, I had been away from my normal station for well over an hour. Taff was due to play in the uckers semi-final, so I went to relieve him. The boat, meanwhile, continued to run at periscope depth with that and the snort mast raised at about two feet above the oggin and the 'old man' taking the opportunity now to snort and generate power in our batteries via the diesel engines. This meant that any fresh air that was surplus to requirements for the diesels would now be distributed, much to our communal gratitude, throughout the boat. This process, known as 'snorting', was not without risk in the area we were in but it was something that had to be done, even if the chances of us being detected by enemy radar was considerable as we were doing so. But it was a risk we regularly had to take as, without battery power, we were neither use nor ornament. At least though, during these procedures we could afford to relax a little bit – after all, if someone wanted to know we were out there during this time, they didn't need us to be walking around the boat to help them. So we could, at least, be a little more mobile. And yes, the heads could now be visited by all who needed them. Yet we still had to remain alert and, whilst this was going on, ELINT was of paramount importance.

Then things began, slowly, to happen. The boat's HE reported a very faint contact on an unknown bearing. But, after a further ten minutes or so, HE reported that nothing further had been detected and concluded it was a possible overreaction, not at all surprising, given the circumstances and heightened sense of tension that enveloped us. But at least the silence had been broken. Assuming that there was nothing too untoward for us to concern ourselves about, at least for the time being, the 'old man' said he was going to take the boat down to 120 feet so everyone could relax, have a tot and some hard tack (navy biscuits) as the galley was, for the time being, to remain closed. The boat's safety was now in the hands of our navigator whilst the 'old man' took the opportunity to pay a quick visit to the heads himself.

I was staring, as per usual, at my screen, hoping upon hope that some sort of activity would now prevail whilst still wondering if my system was working properly, the small seed of doubt that had been planted in my mind by the 'old man' asking me a little earlier boring away at me. It was something he had probably done out of routine rather than a real concern, but the doubts were still fermenting within me. Then, suddenly, a faint radar emission became apparent on the left of my oscilloscope in an area that I had never witnessed before. At the same time, an equally faint audible signal became apparent. Curious rather than alarmed at this stage, I switched on my tape recorder and waited for something to happen, remembering the words of the GCHQ boffin who had pre-warned us that if we heard anything whilst we were in these waters, it would be 'close, bloody close'. The emission I was picking up was within a frequency spectrum that GCHQ had indicated as an unknown high-definition and very short range radar. That meant that, if anything was out there, then, by definition, it already had to be quite close to us. I could only hope that it wasn't, as yet, 'bloody close'.

The elongated visual display I was using was calibrated in frequency and from left to right, 'Q' band, 'X' band and 'S' band. 'Q' band, which I had seen that faint emission on, operated within a very high-frequency spectrum, meaning that anything we picked up on that band would have been transmitted from a source that was three to four miles away – or closer. Then, as I looked, that same radar contact returned although noise and trace were still weak. It was enough for me.

'Dive, dive, dive!' came from my otherwise silent lips.

I cannot remember shouting 'dive' or even, amongst the anxiety that was prevailing, if I even shouted anything at all. It was, however, later communicated to me that I did, indeed, shout those words.

We crash dived. Doing this was nothing short of suicidal. The snort mast and after periscope were both raised as the diesel engines pounded away, sucking in life-giving air. As we then proceeded to head into the depths, water began pouring into the control room through the snort intake. Fortunately for us, our elephant's trunk (a canvas shute rigged around the conning tower ladder which collected incoming seawater in rough weather) had been rigged so that it would be able to cope with such an event. As we dived, my immediate concern was my aerial feeders. You'll remember how I described earlier that they needed to be gathered up and cradled in my arms whenever the periscope was lowered, else they would snap in two. Fortunately, I was quick enough to gather them all up with my right arm, but did so at the same time as one of the periscope handles clobbered me, full on, across the left shoulder. That hard impact led to my slipping on the now soaking wet and slippery operations room decking, and I ended up sprawled on that hard floor amongst an assortment of chairs, slide rules, pencils, headphones, tins of Kye and a load of cups.

The emergency red lighting now came on, making it extremely difficult, at first, to understand just what the hell was happening. Fortunately, amid all the rough and tumble, I had managed to save the ELINT feeders from being severed. Now, gradually, and as silently as possible, the operations room began to return to something close to normality. We had been lucky, very lucky. The snort mast and periscope were successfully recovered and it soon became apparent that no immediate damage to *Turpin* had occurred. Back in my office, however, as I sat astride my rickety chair, I had my head in my hands and was wondering just what the hell I had done. I was frightened, very frightened, and started to shake, wondering if I had made the right move or even if I was hallucinating. After what seemed an eternity, the 'old man', still in whispering mode, began questioning everyone in the operations room. I didn't know, and still don't, if he was in the ops room when we dived, although I suspect he was. At the time I had shouted 'dive', the navigator was using the periscope and that is probably why it had come down so swiftly.

After he'd finished asking the HE specialist questions, the 'old man' headed my way. I fully expected to be next on his list but no, he walked right past my door. How long he eventually took doing his rounds in the ops room seemed an eternity and I started, as I sat and waited, to quake in my boots, thinking to myself, over and over again, 'What have I done?'. Eventually however, he came into my office, closed the door and, leaning on the bulkhead, quietly asked me, 'What happened?'. I then recited the events of those last few seconds as precisely and clearly as I could whilst, as I did so, my childhood stutter, which few had previously detected, came to the fore with a vengeance. The 'old man' calmed me down and told the yeoman to bring me a cup of one of our most scarce supplies, namely water.

With whispering and restrictive movement ordered, the operations room crew were literally picking up the pieces from the water-soaked deck as we slowly began to return to something near normality. The boat's safety was now squarely on the shoulders of our HE specialist, the sole person the 'old man' could now rely on.

We were now lying quietly at a depth of 120 feet following our rapid and unexpectedly sudden crash dive. Under our keel lay a further 250 feet of very cold saline water, not an awful lot of room in which we could manage any sort of quick and undetected getaway. After what seemed like hours but was more probably a very short time, HE reported a 'possible contact', although it was very weak. A couple of seconds later, HE was much more positive.

'HE bearing green zero four five. Multiple HE closing.'

It was time to listen.

To wait.

And to pray.

The ASDIC pinging which had, at first, come from several different directions and had been fairly loud with it, now started slowly to veer away. It was, of course, coming from a large ship on the surface, possibly a heavily armed Russian cruiser. Thankfully we had not been detected; the very cold water had saved us. The water in the Barents Sea can be very cold indeed, but, as was the case here, that sheer and unremitting cold can be more than helpful as it can lead to false echoes or echoes that can be very difficult to obtain a bearing of with any degree of accuracy. Cold layers of water often aid the hunted by 'bending' the pulse going towards and returning from the contact – in this case, *Turpin*. This does, of course, also work the other way around, something that can bring as much frustration to the hunter as it does sheer relief for the hunted. Pinging from a surface ship that hits a submarine is frightening enough but, when it comes from several ships at the same time, the noise is, shall we say, rather alarming! Fortunately, I may not have been as frightened as some of the crew were as, to me, the ASDIC pings were reassuring.

I knew their presence meant I had made the right decision, something which gave me a lot of confidence. As for my sudden and loud outburst, the 'old man' never mentioned it; all he ever said to me when we returned to *Dolphin* was 'Well done,' with a slight tap on the shoulder.

Whilst we were lying at 120 feet, I played back my tape recording in order to begin analysing the 'Q' band intercept. This confirmed to me that the frequency was indeed in the 'Q' band and that the transmission we detected was from a beamed radar rather than a rotating radar; for example, the beamed radar that comes from a guided mission control system which, of course, it may well have been. To my immense satisfaction, GCHQ later confirmed that my intercept was the radar signal that was at the top of their 'most wanted' list.

Later on, as I stood at the bottom of the gangway of *Turpin* and about to leave, wobbly of leg and unable to stand without aid, the coxswain gave me a dolphin badge, set as a pair of dolphins, something which every submariner wears above his medals and with a lot of pride. Whilst I was still serving, however, I was unable to wear my dolphins without the possibility of drawing some unwanted attention, something which would, in time, have invited some rather embarrassing questions which, inevitably in those days might have contravened the Official Secrets Act (OSA). Today, sixty-odd years since diesel electric stretched 'T' boats ceased the operations outlined here and 43 years after I left the Royal Navy, the OSA no longer applies.

Today, when I am hunting for matching cufflinks in my 'jewellery drawer', my dolphin badge appears with hopeful regularity as if it is saying to me, 'It's about time you clipped me in your jacket above your Cold War medal.'

Our brush with a possible international incident on one hand or, on the other, our demise, had come and gone. We were now on our way home, a trip that, with the notable exception of the crash dive, turned out to be one of the quietest I had ever experienced.

In hindsight, I wonder what fabrication would have been concocted by our illustrious leaders if *Turpin* had either been sunk or, perhaps more to the point, politely asked to accompany a pair of Kotlin-class destroyers into custody at Kola? Would we have been treated to a slap-up meal and been offered some first-class Russian hospitality before being sent home in receipt of a gentle telling-off from a Russian vice-admiral? I doubt it. Your guess is as good as mine as to what would have happened to us if *Turpin* had been captured, but it's fair to say that neither we nor our submarine would have ever set out for home. The British press would, of course, have had the proverbial field day to end all field days. But whatever they claimed might have happened, our predicament would, doubtless, have been denied by the government and we would have been left to our own devices. I often think about this and, whenever I do, the tragic case of the trawler *Gaul* readily comes to mind.

What did have far longer repercussions, certainly for me, was being clobbered, as I was, by the one-and-a-half-ton handle of the periscope. The incident had left me in a lot of pain and had considerably restricted my mobility. I had, up to that time, been extremely fit so suddenly being unable to even move around and perform my day to day duties without feeling some discomfort was enormously distressing to me and not just in a physical sense as it affected me mentally as well.

Several months after this trip, I was addressed by the captain of HMS *Mercury*. He told me that he knew little to nothing about what had taken place or, indeed, where it had happened or how, but he had been informed that 'something' had happened to me on that trip by my boss, Lieutenant Commander 'Chips' Selby-Bennett RN. He congratulated me for doing 'whatever it was that you did' and, in doing so, awarded me six months' advancement to chief petty officer. He also said that I had been recommended for the British Empire Medal (BEM), giving me the option of receiving the award at that time or waiting until I was older and letting it go, at this time, to one of the chief petty officers who'd served on both *Turpin* and *Totem* who was shortly due to leave the service. I felt, I have to admit, under a little pressure at this point, as all of this had come completely out of the blue to me. So, standing there with him and in front of the captain, I agreed to wait for my award. In the meantime, I had also been awarded a commendation, duly appended to the award board. The captain also asked me if I would like to accept a new posting in Hong Kong, which I did. I later learned that the intercepted radar which I had recorded and analysed was the first known contact of a new

Russian radar operating on such a high frequency. Had I not made the decision that I did at the time I first picked up that signal then, as I was later made aware, it is more than likely that *Turpin* would have ended up somewhere that we would never have wanted to go.

CHAPTER 8

Sputnik

'I was, by now, desperately trying to fathom out the purpose of this new and completely unfamiliar moving noise.'

If my mission on *Turpin* had to remain top secret, my next close encounter with new Soviet technology took place at a much more public event. During my time in Hong Kong, the moment that marked the pinnacle of my time in the Royal Navy was achieved: the day I located and tracked the recently launched *Sputnik 1*.

Sputnik 1 (the word *sputnik* translates as 'travelling companion') was the first ever artificial satellite sent into orbit around the Earth. It was launched by the Soviet Union on October 4th 1957, a polished metal sphere 23 inches in diameter with four external radio antennas which were used to broadcast radio pulses. The successful launch and flight of *Sputnik 1* came at the height of the Cold War and landed a tremendous political and psychological blow to the United States government of that time, ushering in the Space Race as well as new political, military, technological and scientific developments.

It was, without doubt, one of the most significant moments in the history of our planet.

The success of *Sputnik 1* led, naturally, to a great deal of consternation in the United States. The USA had long regarded themselves as the world leaders in all matters scientific and technological (even if much of the progress they had made in the science of rocketry had been down to Werner Von Braun, an exiled German) only to find itself usurped by a nation who they'd comfortably 'beaten' in the race to build (and use) the first ever atomic bomb. The Soviet Union had tested their first nuclear weapon in 1949 and now, less than a decade later, seemed to have the capability to deliver a nuclear warhead directly to any major US city from space. This led to a number of protective initiatives being put into place, including the famous 'duck and cover' programme. But, even as the US public were being advised how to protect themselves in the event of a nuclear attack, their government and military were working on how to send missiles of their own down onto Soviet Bloc centres of population.

The era of 'mutually assured destruction' had begun and the Cold War was hotting up. The British military had detonated their first atomic bomb in 1952 which meant that, like it or not, we were now as vulnerable to space-borne attack as the USA was. Which meant that now, five years later, I was, like everyone else, expected to play a small role in working out how best to thwart the designs of this new and dangerous enemy.

At around that time, my team of four Radio Warfare specialists were set to join the Royal Navy New Zealand HMNZS *Royalist* which was diverting to Hong Kong, where I'd departed HMT *Navasa* in order to pick us up. We soon learned that, upon joining the ship, we would be sailing to Japan, although no reason for this was known or forthcoming.

Throughout the twelve years that had passed since the end of the Second World War, the *Royalist* and its sister ship, *Black Prince*, had been sitting at their berths in a New Zealand harbour, waiting to find out what, in a changing world, their ultimate fates would be. *Royalist* had originally been a ship of our own Royal Navy that had been leased to New Zealand in 1956, staying in service for a decade afterwards. She, along with *Black Prince*, had been waiting to see what their post-war role in the Pacific Ocean would be. The crew knew, at this point, that it involved the trip to Japan. The reason that they were diverting to Hong Kong to take on a quartet of Brits was, as yet, unknown – to them and to us although, for me, sailing into the unknown was now what I was used to.

The Cold War was at its peak. Quite what would have happened had *Turpin*'s foray into Russian waters the previous year been revealed to the Russian navy and Moscow is anyone's guess, although, as I wrote in the last chapter, it would probably have ended up with the *Turpin* and all the crew disappearing forever and a concocted story from the Navy and HM Government to try to explain it. At least now, en route to Japanese waters, we were not on such a potentially dangerous mission. The Japanese were, of course, a wartime enemy but that time was past and attempts at restoring cordial relations between Britain and Japan were already under way.

As soon as we boarded *Royalist*, we handed a large, sealed brown envelope to the captain. This had originated in the office of the commander-in-chief of the Far East Fleet in Singapore and was classified SECRET.

Within this envelope were several smaller sealed envelopes, each and every one of which possessed an alphabetical sign. The outside of the large envelope gave instructions for the captain to open and pass the contents to the Radio Warfare team when instructed to do so by the commander-in-chief. It soon became clear that these instructions, whatever they were, had come from GCHQ. Any communications had to be made directly to Singapore Wireless by high-frequency communications channels before switching to more traditional landline (albeit in code) to reach the Admiralty in London who, in turn, would pass the message to GCHQ in Cheltenham, again via landline.

During our passage from Hong Kong, it soon became clear that Asian flu had, somehow, been carried on board the ship as several members of the crew, together with a number of the New Zealand rugby team, who were sailing with us as guests for a visit to Japan, were reporting sick. Our sick bay was, as a result, soon full and we had to find extra room on the ship for the growing number of casualties. This meant that, upon our arrival at Sasebo, the major port of the Japanese navy, we were obliged to hoist the yellow duster, a visual sign that indicated to all and sundry that we had a contagious disease on board and all were to keep well clear of us.

This presented a few problems. We were, for example, running short of basic foodstuffs. Discussions were held with authorities from the USA who, at that time, were still administering Japan and, eventually, we were sent supplies of what we had asked for – in this case, water, milk, fresh fruit and vegetables and the like. It had, however, to be winched on board and no members of the shore-side team were to be involved in the procedure at all. In addition, no one was allowed on or off the ship, even though we had a dangerously ill and contagious member of crew still in the sick bay. We were, it seemed, at the disease's mercy with no chance of escape.

Thankfully, within a couple of days, the sick crew member was sitting up in bed and talking. The entire crew of *Royalist* were, as you might guess, elated at this news, especially when he had his tot, something which mysteriously made its way to his bedside along with a few further 'gulpers', courtesy of his mates! The situation began to ease soon after that and we'd been at Sasebo for about six days when the order came through for the main envelope to be opened. The message in this one instructed the captain to leave Sasebo and to head northwards up through the Sea of Japan at economical speed. Fortunately, the sea state was calm which helped and, following three days of plain sailing, we were only a few hundred miles off the far eastern coast of Russia with the only activity encountered en route a few fishing trawlers, the largest of which just happened to be festooned with radio aerials!

The next envelope due to be opened was Envelope November. The contents instructed me to set watch on a given frequency. I was initially doubtful about the practicality of tuning into this frequency and asked *Royalist*'s captain for clarification after finding it was jammed tight with all sorts of radio noises from a variety of sources that just happened to operate in the band given. GCHQ were in touch with us within half an hour of this query, confirming that yes, the frequency given in these sealed instructions had been the correct one. I conveyed this information onto my operators but we ended up finding the task a bit of a farce with that given frequency constantly saturated with single- and double-side band emissions as well as the dreaded weather balloon traffic which, at times, was so dominant, it blotted everything else out.

I left my leading telegraphist in charge of operations in order for me to be able to slip below for my tot and dinner, leaving one of the wireless receivers switched to loud speaker. Soon after I'd finished my meal and headed back to my office, I began to hear, amidst all the tremendous clatter, a new and unfamiliar transmission. Tuning into this new noise correctly, my leading telegraphist told me it had just been singled out and put on the tape recorder before becoming fainter again as the minutes passed, then returning, over an hour later.

Looking at the signal on an oscilloscope (an instrument commonly used to capture, process, display and analyse the waveform and bandwidth of electronic signals), I noticed what appeared to be several squares with some sort of information within each. When the signal returned, it, once again, increased to an almost deafening force five before varying in fainter degrees until it disappeared once again. This moving transmission was rotating, according to our observations, once every hour or so.

I was, by now, desperately trying to fathom out the purpose of this new and completely unfamiliar moving noise.

Our next instruction required us, once we had made our notes and recordings, to send a secret codeword to Singapore, which we did. We heard nothing more until the following day when we heard on the BBC Overseas News that the Soviet Union had launched the first ever artificial satellite into Earth orbit. It was *Sputnik 1* whose distinctive radio signal we had heard as it made its lonely orbit around the Earth.

It also meant that the Americans had been beaten into the space age.

CHAPTER 9

HMS *Devonshire*

'Why, I kept asking myself, *why* had I been thrown out of the branch that
I loved so much and shoved into one that I hated – yes, hated.'

I joined HMS *Devonshire* in October 1966 as the ship's master-at-arms
(MAA).

HMS *Devonshire* was the first of the County-class (a guided missile
destroyer) ships in the Royal Navy. Built by Cammell Laird in Birkenhead,
it had a displacement of 5,440 tonnes (6,850 tonnes full load). *Devonshire*
was named after the English county of Devon and was launched on June
10th 1960 before being delivered to the Royal Navy two years later. It
was, therefore, still a relatively new ship when I joined in October 1966.

I'd joined as an MAA with responsibilities that included maintaining
discipline and leave as well as keeping the second-in-command, namely
the ship's executive commander, fully appraised of all matters that concern
the lower deck. The MAA is the senior member of the lower deck,
irrespective of how long he has held that particular rank, and is the most
senior non-commissioned officer in the regulating branch.

Devonshire had a complement of 440 men, a total which included fifteen
officers of various rank from midshipman up to captain. The captain,
when I joined, was a well-liked and much respected senior Navy man,
as was the second in command. My immediate predecessor had departed
the ship before I arrived and I later learned that the MAA originally
designated to take his place had withdrawn, which meant that I was the
replacement for him.

On the deck of HMS *Devonshire* (courtesy Tony Beasley)

A directive had recently been issued by the Admiralty decreeing that an MAA should serve on every seagoing ship as a replacement for the coxswain who presently undertook that position. The only sea-going post for an MAA up until this time was on an aircraft carrier, something that entailed a totally different life than anything else in the Royal Navy. MAAs throughout the service were thought to be up in arms over this directive. They had had an expectation of a relatively cushy life onboard an aircraft carrier or in one of the many shore bases the Navy had throughout the world until they retired with their pension. The cessation of all of this therefore came as somewhat of a shock to them all in 1965.

Many complaints and threats of resignation were made, fuelled by the officer in charge of the regulating school, a 'passed over' lieutenant commander. His own aspirations of becoming the first commander in the regulating branch had not come about as he was now considered beyond his sell-by date for a number of reasons. It was this particular officer who made my own transfer to regulating branch, something that was made even more difficult by his ignoring an Admiralty directive that stated I should make a straight transfer from my senior position of chief radio supervisor (Electronic Warfare) to a master-at-arms. I've little doubt that his ire was heightened by the fact that I hadn't made the move in the time-honoured way and was therefore seen as an unwelcome interloper.

This particular directive, however, came from the very top and was made for a reason that I was bound by the Official Secrets Act not to discuss. Despite that, the issue clearly upset this particularly impertinent and unreasonable officer, the like of which I had never experienced in my twenty-four years' service in the Royal Navy.

At this time, *Devonshire*'s long-awaited future deployment was still not known to the ship's company. There had been numerous 'buzzes' flying around the ship; these were beginning to get out of hand and had been made even more outlandish by the occasional 'Andy Capp' cartoons that were appearing on the ship's notice boards, all depicting possible destinations with pictures of objects such as boomerangs, coco-de-mers (a rare species of palm tree native to the Seychelles archipelago in the Indian Ocean) and geisha girls. Quite where the buzzes originated were anyone's guess but, as it later turned out, some of these assumptions were absolutely spot on.

At around about this time, our beloved captain was selected for promotion to flag rank and retired from the ship with his replacement swiftly appointed and sent out to us. HMS *Devonshire* was, at this time, coming to the end of a refit in Devonport dockyard, which was its home port, although the majority of the ship's company were based in Portsmouth. It had been generally believed over the years that, within the senior service, there was an 'interested party' in the drafting depot at Gosport, HMS *Centurion* – a man who was responsible for drafting ships' companies to ships and either owned or was in cahoots with the owners of the halfway stopping-off point at Bridport in Dorset. Here, it was not unknown for dozens of coaches, all packed to the gunnels with Portsmouth men, to stop every week en route from Portsmouth to Devonport or vice versa. This handy little stopping-off point was, not surprisingly, very popular with legions of thirsty matelots, all eager to stretch their legs and buy a cup of tea. The rumours therefore had it that the owner of this particular café must have been a very wealthy ex-admiral who now spent his time ripping off sailors and making money out of men whose only objective on the day was to see their loved ones and to get away from the grime, filth and noise that were so abundant in Royal Naval dockyards.

When ships were being refitted there was at least some effort made to accommodate the ship in question's company ashore. More often than not, this was not possible. Having, as a result of this, to put up with all the resultant noise, clamour and dust of a refit for weeks on end was enough to drive absolutely anyone to drink, as a ship's punishment return would inevitably show. But what bugged the crew of HMS *Devonshire* more than anything was that, time after time, when weekend leave could have been granted, it was not. As the ship's MAA, responsible, amongst other things, for managing leave, I could not understand why men who were not required for duty were obliged to remain on board for no apparent reason, especially as a long and very hard six-week work-up at Portland was looming. Such a completely unnecessary leave restriction was to become part of the cause for otherwise disciplined men going absent without leave, transgressions that inevitably led to periods of detention for those involved.

Many of these otherwise very well trained and conscientious men who had years and years of experience between them ended up leaving the service. They did this either by buying themselves out or being discharged as Services No Longer Required (SNLR). I suspect that many of them had been 'working their ticket' (deliberately doing things wrong so that their superiors would eventually tire of them and their methods and discharge them) in order to get out. It was clear to me that HMS *Devonshire*, which had once been a very happy ship, was floundering – and the reasons for this were now abundantly clear.

The assignment out to Portland came ever closer, my first with *Devonshire*. I knew Portland well, having undergone several periods of time there during my role as the Squadron Electronic Warfare specialist (previously Radio Warfare) where I had been responsible for each of the four ships within my squadron, all of which would often be separated from each other by a distance of many miles. It was just one of countless places I travelled to in the line of work – Londonderry, Rosyth, Chatham, Portsmouth and Devonport included, training staff and calibrating equipment at each of them. I had loved the job and the work but, of course, having to do so much travelling and be away from home for so much time meant that my private life with my wife and three children suffered.

Prior to leaving for the work we needed to do at Portland, the long-awaited news concerning *Devonshire's* longer-term future programme was finally confirmed. Christmas would be spent in Cape Town before we would head north and up the east coast of Africa to the Seychelles, home of the aforementioned coco-de-mer. Sydney, Singapore, Hong Kong and Sasebo (Japan) were also on the itinerary, the sort of cruise that was otherwise known as 'showing the flag'. It was certainly something we could all look forward to. Beforehand, however, one rather large hurdle remained. We still had to get through our six-week work-up at Portland, something which was in no way a rubber-stamped walkover. For a change though, the weather wasn't too bad which did make life on board ship at least a little bit more bearable.

It soon became apparent, however, that certain sections of the ship were not knitting together as well as the work-up team required, with some department 'rescrubs' (roughly defined as 'do it again and do it better') ending up taking up valuable time and adding extra strain onto the ship's company as a whole. As a consequence of this, by the halfway stage of our stay at Portland, the crew were, not to put too fine a point on it, completely knackered. This led to buzzes appearing on the ship's notice boards claiming that our round-the-world jaunt 'showing the flag' cruise might even be called off. A member of the work team later told me that the weak point of the ship was the chain of command from the captain downwards. I wasn't at all surprised to hear this. Had it not been for the valuable experience shown by the chief petty officers in charge of their individual departments, the ship would have been given a total rescrub rather than it having to happen in certain departments. This had happened before but, thanks to them, it didn't on this occasion. Once again the words of the onetime Admiral of the Fleet, Lord Louis

HMS *Devonshire* – life in the mess (1960) (courtesy Tony Beasley)

Mountbatten – 'My ships are run by my chief petty officers and petty officers' – were in my mind. Lord Louis was an honorary life member of the Royal Naval Communication Chiefs' Association (RNCCA) of which I am a former secretary.

The difficulty with the chain on command on *Devonshire* can be summed up as follows. Overall responsibility for a ship lies squarely on the shoulders of the ship's captain, he that wears the four gold rings on his uniform. Next in command is the executive officer, a commander who wears three gold rings. All the other officers on board the ship are junior to both these officers within the ship, irrespective of their own seniority within their relative branch. However, in the case of *Devonshire* two additional recently promoted commanders joined the ship, one of whom was a supply branch (S&S) officer who had overall responsibility for victuals – food, spares, paperwork and the like. It was rumoured that he was a barrister and his arrogance certainly portrayed him as such.

The other was an engineer branch officer. Both officers, in their specific rank of commander, were surplus to requirements and, upon promotion, should have been replaced with the proper ship's rank entitlement, that is a lieutenant commander. This would have allowed the executive officer, the man appointed to serve immediately below the captain, to carry out his duties without interference.

Sadly, this turned out not to be the case.

It meant that there was more than one person with the rank equivalent of executive officer on board the ship. This is something that the captain should have noticed, as should the officers' appointee in the Admiralty. I had, on several occasions, gone to see the executive commander in his cabin, as was my duty, but couldn't help but hear the arguments raging between him and the S&S commander which I found most embarrassing. Fortunately, only a few other members of the ship's company passed the executive commander's cabin, so not that many people got to hear the rumpus that was going on behind those very firmly shut doors.

Devonshire had endured more than its fair share of problems with the diesel G6 gas turbine engines which were repeatedly giving us cause for concern. The engineer CPOs, who were extremely skilled technicians, were constantly briefing the engineering commander on what he should be telling the captain. As an officer, this man was just a mouthpiece, a go-between and a totally unnecessary one. It was no different to a cabinet minister being told what to do by a civil servant.

***

Work done, HMS *Devonshire* did spend the Christmas of 1967 in Cape Town. We received a very cordial reception upon our arrival, one that was afforded to the entire ship's company. Following our stopover there, the next port of call for the ship was Mahe on the island of Victoria, the capital of the Seychelles. Getting there meant traversing the notorious Agulhas current, the second fastest in the world, which swept down the Mozambique Channel at a fair rate of knots. This was a location where many ships that chose to hug the South African coast too closely ended up floundering with disastrous consequences. A ship that comes to mind with regard to this is HMS *Birkenhead*. This was a two-masted sail and steamship which was caught in the Agulhas current whilst sailing, too close as it turned out, to the mainland. As a result of this, the *Birkenhead* hit a rock and capsized. The story, tragic as it is, became all the more famous when it became known how the soldiers that were sailing on board at the time all stood fast in order to allow all the women and children to use the lifeboats. Of the 600 men who were on board, only around 190 survived. The *Birkenhead* was also carrying nine horses, eight of which were able to swim ashore. The well-known phrase 'women and children first' originated with this maritime disaster.

Our visit to the Seychelles was meant to last for three days. However, due to an incident which involved *Devonshire*'s bottom becoming over-familiar with a coral reef as we entered Mahe harbour, our stay was extended. Not that we would experience any home comforts during our visit as we didn't expect, and didn't get, any mail from home whilst we were there – hardly surprising as Mahe had no airport, although this changed many years later. We did, however, receive fresh green food, milk and water as well as other vital supplies. Our speed was then reduced to ten knots, meaning that our onward trip from Mahe to Sydney would now take around three weeks. That long haul turned out to be a bit of a slog. Boredom soon became a major issue amongst the ship's company, myself included. To try and alleviate this, I asked the captain if I could assist the navigator on the bridge, or act as the second officer of the watch. I had some previous knowledge of both these responsible positions, having assisted on the bridge of the troopship HMT *Navasa* en route to Hong Kong as we sailed around the Cape of Good Hope in 1957. Much to my surprise, the captain of *Devonshire* agreed to my request. My addition to the watch sequence also helped out the junior officers, who normally carried out these duties, as they were now able to have a little more time off.

For the first seven or eight days of the trip, there was little to do apart from count the dolphins and porpoises that were appearing in ever-increasing numbers as they played at the bows of the ship. We were also entertained by flying fish that would, all too often, end up on our helicopter deck before being picked up and consumed by the more adventurous members of our crew. Both of our radar screens were clear which only added to the monotony. The most you could expect was pacing up and down the bridge with, very occasionally, an interruption as our long-range 'S' band radar picked up an airborne contact that would have not only been flying at a very high altitude but was many hundreds of miles away.

We eventually had some company and something to talk about, however: forging our way through the waters of the southern ocean, a most inhospitable place at the best of times, we located George, found by one of our 'X' band navigational radars one miserably wet and very choppy forenoon. George was a splendid wandering albatross.

During his time with us, George, given that name so his movements could be written in the ship's log, became an interesting pastime for everyone on board. He may well have been, of course, a Georgina, but who cares? Thus we'd hear information passed out to the next officer of the watch (OOW) along the lines of 'George bearing green zero four five' or similar, there being little else, apart from the weather, to record. On a couple of occasions, when the weather was a little tough, for example, a force nine or ten blowing up from Antarctica, he would alight on our helicopter deck and cadge a lift under one of the leeward sea boats. He refused, point blank, the shelter of our helicopter hangar and would get very stroppy with anyone who might think they were doing him a good turn.

At one stage, George managed to wrap a wing around part of the decking, displaying, in the process, just how strong and large this gentle giant of the southern ocean was. Speculation stirred on the mess deck that, with all the food that the crew were putting out for him, George wouldn't be able to take off when he needed to; yet, when land was eventually picked up by our radar on the port quarter, our splendid passenger took off easily. Facing into the wind and making a couple of effortless flaps of his enormous wings, he was airborne, up and away, remaining over the ship until our helicopter took off. A gigantic and wonderful travelling companion who, despite his apparent fondness for our company would, nonetheless, resist all human interference. That didn't stop him, however, from being the subject of several mysterious drawings that appeared from time to time on the ship's notice boards and he featured prominently, together with some other questionable cartoons. George took his final leave of us as we approached Albany, a small town on the south-west coast of Australia where we were due to pick up some much-looked-forward-to mail as well as collect fresh supplies of vegetables, fruit and water.

True to form however, the regulating staff at BFPO Ships had redirected all of our mail to Sydney instead of Albany, with the former still being at least another week away. This meant that we hadn't received any mail since leaving Cape Town, a wait now of well over six weeks. Perhaps the staff back in London had briefly glanced at a map of Australia and deduced that Sydney was 'only an inch or so' from Albany; near enough, for them, to make the decision to forward everything to Sydney. An inch or two on a map maybe but, in real life, a distance of around 1,818 nautical miles which, at a speed of just ten knots, would take us over another week to achieve. This neglect in forwarding our mail properly added to the general contempt that was held for the regulating branch – a feeling that, I hasten to add, was richly deserved. A ship's company that is at sea for any length of time without mail is one that will inevitably find itself in trouble that, more often than not, will lead to courts martial. On one occasion, for example, a 'sit down' in the stokers' mess deck occurred which could have turned nasty had it not been for the very able regulating chief petty officer, a stalwart if ever there was one, who was able to sort things out without any interference.

It was around about the time of the stokers' actions that a midshipman came to see me, one who, as he arrived in my office, looked to be physically upset. I locked my office door and we talked, it very soon became clear that his concerns related not to himself but to one of the ship's senior officers. Now, this particular midshipman, or 'Middy', was a well-liked officer who got on well with the rest of the crew and he went onto tell me that he was getting so worked up about things, he was toying with the idea of resigning from the service. I shared with him my own concerns about the officer in question which may, I hope, have helped him—and perhaps it did, for he stayed in the service and rose up to become a much-respected Captain RN.

Much of the buzz about the ship as well as the subject of some of the cartoons that jostled for space with those of George on the notice board featured this particular officer, and this was the reason for the Midshipman's concern. I had, at around this time, been elected as the ship's 'school master', a privilege that saw me reap an extra two shillings a day in pay. Fresh events and rumours circulating about the officer soon found their way to me and after one alleged event was passed onto me by the ship's Quartermaster, I tried to maintain calm and some sense of order on the ship by treating it all as a storm in a tea cup, even though my duties required me to mention what I had heard to the Executive Officer, which is what I did. Another buzz raging around the ship surrounded another member of the ship's company who was absent over leave whilst the ship was under sailing orders. This was most unusual as no-one could ever absent themselves without leave as, almost without exception, the outcome would include his being reduced in rank or privileges. What was even more unusual was that this appalling lack of discipline was being shown by someone whose duties included installing discipline into the ship's company.

When we finally arrived in Sydney we picked up the long-awaited bag of mail that had seemingly been following us halfway around the world for the last few weeks. Its arrival meant that the mood of the ship's company now changed to one of happiness and jubilation – with one notable exception, that of a crew member who received a 'Dear John' letter which brought him such sadness and despair, he was eventually granted compassionate leave so that he could fly home.

Whilst we were in Sydney, I took a few days' (official!) leave so that I could visit my sister who was living in Dee Why, about 12 miles north-east of the city. Soon after I arrived back on board however, I could feel a distinct aura of trouble as the previously absent crew member had arrived back on the ship and was now a major talking point amongst the ship's company. Much of the talk, unsurprisingly, centred on what might end up being done about him missing the ship in the Seychelles as doing so when your ship is under sailing orders is a very serious offence. As the MAA, I could only look at it in that way and knew that he would have to be treated in exactly the same way as any seaman who might

Naval paperwork in my office (courtesy Tony Beasley)

have erred in the same way. It was all very straightforward as far as I was concerned and there wouldn't be any problems getting on with what I had to do and dealing with both him and the situation.

But there were.

Because of what was afoot, the next leg of the ship's journey, sailing from Sydney to Singapore was a very tense one as no decision seemed to be even pending with regard to what action to take against the previously absent crew member. This delay resulted in more cartoons appearing on the ship's notice boards, the theme now being this individual as well as the officer I have already mentioned. Yet, as if this wasn't enough, that trip to Singapore saw my life turned upside down for a totally different reason, something which, in hindsight, was entirely my own doing. My cabin was opposite the electronic war office (EWO) which, on many of the ships I had previously served upon, had been my domain. I had, before entering my cabin on *Devonshire*, often stood and stared towards this office before shutting my cabin door behind me and sitting down with my head in my hands, trying to come to terms as to why I had been thrown out of a job that I loved so much, into one that I loathed and felt very uncomfortable in.

Electronic Warfare was my life. Yet it had been snatched away from me by some fledgling RN medical officer (MO) who didn't know me from Adam. Because I had historically suffered from slight mood swings and sometimes stuttered, the latter being something which I had put up with since I was eight, this MO had considered me a security risk. Not being able to work at what I had not only trained to do but was exceptionally good at and enjoyed was something which repeatedly got me down during my time on *Devonshire* as I could not believe the logic behind my being 'removed' (as I saw it, it was never a voluntary step) from performing the duties I both loved and enjoyed. It was certainly something which occupied my mind a great deal during my 'down time' and it was on such an afternoon that my thoughts were interrupted by a knock on my cabin door. I duly opened it to find the chief radio supervisor (CRS(S)) standing there. He was in charge of the EWO opposite my cabin. Puzzled, I invited him in and we sat down and talked. I couldn't help but notice that he looked worried and, at first, I thought he was seeking my advice on a totally different subject – it wasn't unusual for any of the ship's company to come and see me for a variety of reasons.

But, much to my surprise, he asked me if I would give him the once-over on the equipment in his office as a large-scale exercise was looming during the ship's passage to Japan. I was flabbergasted, as we had both previously been warned that under no circumstances was I to be allowed into the Electronic Warfare office.

In the past, when inspections were being made in this particular part of the ship, I was required to wait outside and not enter before the inspecting officer as I did elsewhere on the ship. But I had, nevertheless, been very surprised when this CRS(S), who I knew, had joined the ship. He was a Russian linguist and had only a limited knowledge of the ELINT side of the branch, something he freely admitted to, adding, just after he had joined, that senior ELINT supervisors were now in very short supply. Now, here was I, an ELINT chief radio supervisor (warfare) who had instructed specialists in the subject for a number of years, still serving, and now doing so on a modern warship but doing the most mundane work in the Royal Navy, being asked to share my experience with someone who should never have been sent to the ship in the first place.

I asked if anyone had put him up to asking me. He said that wasn't the case and he knew that if even asking me the question became general knowledge around the ship, he'd be in serious trouble. I believed him. Yet, although he knew I could bring a very serious charge up against him for making the suggestion, he also knew that I would not do that. And, what's more, I decided to go along with his suggestion. Now, years later, I cannot help but wonder if this was all a put-up job.

As no one was around, we took the opportunity to dart the few feet out of my cabin, across the corridor and into his office. Then, with the door secured behind us, my conducted tour started. At first glance, it seemed as if little had changed since my departure from the branch. On penetrating the room further, however, I noticed that there were two new radar receiving consoles in place. Overall though, the equipment fitted was not that different from the original layout. Exploring a little further, I must, in the process, have let out some sort of audible exclamation of surprise which drew his attention to me and made him aware of what I was glaring at. Trying, as much as I could, to control my emotions, I explained that 'this and this', fingering two operator controls, were based on modifications that I had developed and introduced and, in the process, received a Herbert Lott prize (an 'in-house' RN scheme awarded for good ideas and ingenuity) of £57 10s!

Calming down, I gave a rundown on how to use this and all of the other equipment, aware, as I did so, of a deep sense of emotion building up inside me. Once my conducted tour was over, I retreated to the solace of my cabin and literally went to pieces. This was the nearest I have ever come to topping myself. The weather was ideal: pitch black, blowing a gale and very rough. No one could possibly be held to blame. Why, I kept asking myself, *why* had I been thrown out of the branch that I loved so much and shoved into one that I hated – yes, hated. The only reason I had agreed to the change in the first place was to complete time in order to get a full pension.

Without a shadow of doubt, I was heading for a breakdown.

***

Upon our arrival in Singapore, the tension was, for me, broken, when I was summoned to the gangway to find another sister (I have four) and her husband waiting to see me. As we were due to sail the following day for Hong Kong, I went home with them to their married quarters at RAF Changi and stayed the night, which also gave me the chance to meet my one-year-old niece for the first time. Frolicking in the garden with Nicola on my shoulders, I was suddenly disorientated by a sharp pain across my shoulders. It was so intense, I nearly dropped her as I stumbled into a frangipani tree, from which a white fluid entered my eye. The pain was excruciating

Arriving back on board at 0730 the next morning, I felt it wise to visit the ship's doctor in case I needed eye drops, as had been suggested by my sister. This turned out to be an unwise move, as I later found out to my detriment. I told the doctor about the sap from the tree getting into my eyes, plus the pain across my shoulders. This pain had been ongoing and wasn't a symptom that was unknown to me as I'd previously had several sleepless nights due to it, something he was aware of. Carrying my niece on my shoulders had triggered it again. As we talked, our conversation turned to the main talking point on board – the two members of the ship's crew who had been the focus for much discussion over the previous few weeks. The doctor then changed the subject in hand onto me and mentioned that he thought I was very run down. He was, again in hindsight, correct, but not for the reasons he thought and I certainly wasn't going to mention the rush of emotions that had been brought on by my visit to the Electronic Warfare Office.

Later on, in my still confused state, I recall being outside the Captain's cabin when the subject of the crew member missing the ship was being raised by the officers within. I soon gathered that the reason he was probably not to be charged was that he had made it known that, given a court martial, the RPO would bring up the misdemeanour alleged to have been committed by the officer that had since evolved into the subject of those notice board cartoons.

The humiliation I suffered when a Chief Petty Officer was instructed to strip my cabin and pack my belongings without my being present is, even now, totally beyond my comprehension. I was medically unfit, a condition that had been caused by the incident upon *Turpin* yet was now being treated like a criminal. I could not believe it. Personal belongings within the Regulating Office were never forwarded to me: letters, small change, stamps and a watch were just some of the items. Everything now happened very quickly. Within two days, I was flown home with a medical escort and spent two weeks in Haslar Royal Navy Hospital and Netley Military Hospital before being discharged. I was informed that I was 'run down' and required rest although, at no time was I given a detailed medical or indeed an X-Ray for my shoulders, both, or even either of which, could have completely changed my life. I remain convinced that I was shunted off *Devonshire* in case a court martial was convened against the Captain so my medical misfortune ended up being an incredible opportunity for him. Again, I believe the S&S Commander was directly responsible in his capacity as a 'barrister', and that he had put the idea to the Captain.

I have, of course, no proof. Only instinct. Which is a forte of mine.

At the time, 'run down' was probably the correct diagnosis and the reasons for it are sufficiently described here.

Some years later, whilst watching Meridian television, I witnessed the demise of HMS *Devonshire*. The torpedo which sank her, fired from a British warship, hit the starboard side midships, exactly where my cabin was. They say stranger things have happened.

Of all the ships I served in during my 24-year career, *Devonshire* glaringly shone as the worst.

And by some considerable distance.

CHAPTER 10

A War Pension

'As strategies go, it was a very weak one. But it was sufficient reason for
me to write to him. And it worked.'

I left the Royal Navy on a pension in 1973 at the age of 40. My discharge
card, a 'tick the boxes' type, covered 24 years serving king, queen and
country from 1949 until 1973, said card becoming ever more dishevelled
as it journeyed around the confines of the Royal Naval Barracks at
Portsmouth until, with its being handed in at the main gate, I was, all
of a sudden, a 'free man' once again.

Don't get me wrong. If I could have continued my service, I most
certainly would have done.

But it was a time in my life that now belonged in the past and I was
on my way back to Civvy Street. Fortunately, I wasn't being thrown back
into the maelstrom of 'normal' life completely unprepared, as had been
the case for many others both before and after me. This was because
I'd taken up a franchise with a company that specialised in tuning cars,
something I proceeded to do for a few years until I bought the franchise
out and went out on my own for just over twenty-six years, until my
failing health brought this to a sad conclusion. It wasn't all gloom and
doom at that time, mind you. By then, more and more electronics were
being incorporated into motor vehicle engines which meant that tuning
a modern car required more sophisticated and expensive equipment.
This led to my, reluctantly, giving my ageing Sun Tester machine to a

local man who continues to work on the motor engines of yesteryear. I had, over the preceding years, changed my engine computer six times.

The ongoing pain and discomfort that I had long felt in and around my upper back, shoulders and neck, that had resurfaced with excruciating effect as I'd played with my niece in my sister's garden in Changi, were worsening. The intensity of this was so much so that, on occasions, the pain brought tears to my eyes. I'd long tried to get a diagnosis and treatment for the condition but, from the time I left the Royal Navy in 1973, I had repeatedly been told by service and civilian doctors alike that the problems I was experiencing, the discomfort, aching and painful shoulders and my constantly feeling irritable and depressed as a result of this, were all down to arthritis. I was completely and utterly sick of being fobbed off with the same explanation time and time again, and that may have been as far as I ever got with the issue had I not seen a new GP at my local practice in 1989. She examined me and detected some problems with my neck, advising that I should have an MRI scan. Fortunately, I had private health insurance and arranged for this to be done.

Following my MRI scan I was asked a series of questions.

Could I remember an accident that I might have had in my car or when playing rugby when I was younger? My mind worked overtime but nothing immediately came to mind and all I could offer in response was that my tinnitus, which had also plagued me for many years, was now also becoming a lot more intense and frequent.

Two days afterwards, I woke up after yet another restless night by falling out of bed, ending up in an undignified heap on the floor amidst my bedclothes and books, clearly remembering the dream I had been having before this sudden interruption to my sleep.

The dream had taken me back to my time at HMS *Mercury* in Petersfield and the day I'd joined the Radio Warfare branch of the Royal Navy in 1953, a transfer that I had made in order to avoid service on submarines. It had, of course, turned out to be the one that ultimately saw me serving on one anyway when I, plus Taffy and two others, had joined up with HMS *Turpin* on that cold Sunday morning off Portsmouth in 1955. During my time on *Turpin* I had, during a covert operation in the Barents Sea, suffered that severe neck injury after the heavy fall I sustained as *Turpin* crash dived.

At last, I had a reason for my worsening discomfort and pain.

Because of that injury, I applied for a disability pension, something which is, ambiguously, also called a war pension. You can make an application for it if you suffered an injury or illness as a result of your service in the British Armed Forces before April 6th 2005. So I certainly qualified on that count. Under the war pension scheme, any ex-serviceman or servicewoman can make a claim for any injury or illness which was caused or made worse by their service. This can include minor injuries such as fractures or more serious conditions that include amputations and mental health problems.

It is called a 'war' pension but you do not need to have served in a conflict and there is no time limit to making a claim, although you do have to wait until you have left the service. So all the boxes were very much ticked in my favour. I was confident that, given my service history and the fact that my injury had been directly caused by the aftermath of our crash dive in the Barents Sea when the arms of the periscope had clobbered me on the shoulder, causing me to slip and suffer a heavy fall as a consequence, the acceptance of my claim would be very straightforward.

How wrong I was.

All injuries incurred whilst serving with the military are processed by a branch of the MoD in Blackpool called Norcross NX. This branch is split into two main sections: Officers and Other Ranks respectively. My experience suggests that the MoD's priority in any case that involves an injury to a serviceman or woman is to satisfy the establishment that the injured party was where they say he or she was at the time and that their injury neatly fits into the sequence of events prevailing at the time.

I duly made my application to Norcross NX. It was acknowledged and I was required to forward a Statement of Case (SOC) which had to outline how, where and when the injury to my neck occurred. Fairly straightforward, I thought. As a result of this request, and wholly logically, I typed out an SOC that included the word 'submarines' twice.

Upon receipt of a 'copy' of my typed SOC from NX that I wanted for my files, I was astounded to see that the crucial word 'submarines' had, in both places, been altered to read 'summaries'. Not even subtle! To this day, that glaring alteration has never been corrected, despite my requesting NX to do so on countless occasions. I conclude that this is part of NX's 'wearing down' policy to deter claimants.

As far as NX are concerned, this 'error' is down to their typists. But I do not believe this could possibly be the case. During my early days in the Royal Navy (1949–1952) I became a touch-typing Morse code specialist before, many years later, taking the occasional class of WRNS for touch typing. In no way would a qualified typist make such an error, let alone twice; the placement of the keys makes this sort of thing almost impossible without the typist's prior knowledge or instruction.

NX have, on several occasions, stated that my SOC has been 'carefully considered' – so I now ask, in response, how on earth can a carefully perusing reader help but notice that something within the document is quite patently wrong? The word 'summaries' appears in a sentence twice but, on both occasions, makes absolutely no sense at all. So, for example, how could anyone skip over a sentence that might have read 'I served on a summary'? Of course they wouldn't. It is an insult to the typist to suggest that they might miss it. Nevertheless, that is how it reads and how it was allowed to remain.

Conclusion? NX were lying. The word 'submarines' is at the very crux of my case and without it there is, quite simply, no case.

NX then refused to take any notice when I attempted to explain why 'no references to any connection with submarines were included in my service, medical or pay documents'. These had been intentionally omitted by myself for reasons of security. This was common sense, a term that is seemingly unknown in many MoD circles, something that was further confirmed to me when I worked within a civil service environment at HMS *Centurion* in Gosport during the last of my 24 years of service in the Royal Navy. This was an eye-opening position if ever there was one. Common sense is, I have to say, a gift. It cannot be taught, no matter which school you attended or profession you belong to.

When I advised NX of the day and date that my accident on *Turpin* occurred, they insisted that, on that day, I was serving at the shore establishment at HMS *Mercury* in Petersfield – which is what my service documents showed. NX already knew that this was my administration headquarters at the time, the place from where all covert operations in tandem with GCHQ were conducted. But NX chose not to accept this. Any attempt to convince NX that covert operations were just that – covert and, for that reason, not recorded – was frustrating to say the least.

At another stage, I was told that my service documents were a true appraisal of where and when I had served during my career. Now this is absolute nonsense. I served on at least seven ships, all of which have no connection to the Official Secrets Act, yet, in all seven of those instances, there is no record of my time served aboard them. Such discrepancies became apparent to me during my time 'on loan' to HMS *Centurion*. During my twelve months' service there, I found numerous mistakes and omissions made on service, medical and sometimes even pay documents.

All of this stress and trauma had been building up within me, so much so that, eventually, I became seriously ill, leading to my having to undergo a triple heart bypass operation in October 1994. It was required (and this is fully documented) because I had been living under severe stress. Needless to say, even this professionally given explanation was dismissed by the NX experts who stated that stress does not lead to heart problems. This is, needless to say, in direct contradiction to a report published in the respected weekly peer-reviewed general medical journal *The Lancet*, which is amongst the world's oldest (it was first published in 1823) and most prestigious medical journals. The research, which was published in 2017, claimed to show that constant stress has been linked to higher activity in an area of the brain linked to processing emotions and, as a result, an increased likelihood of the sufferer developing heart and circulatory disease. Confirmation, therefore, of what people had already known for years: stress is bad for your heart!

No it isn't, reckon Norcross.

I fought on. To quote Admiral of the Fleet Lord Terence Lewin after he agreed to assist me in my fight with NX: 'You are one of the three per cent, you will never give in.'

How right he was.

Increasingly desperate, I wrote to the Director of Naval Intelligence (DNI) requesting a visit and an opportunity for further guidance. Within a short time, I was interviewed at my home in Petersfield by a Royal Navy captain, an ex-submarine commander who listened intently to my story. During the interview, which lasted over two hours, the captain said that, although he was in command of a submarine at the time my accident occurred, he never knew what operations *Turpin* and *Totem* were engaged in. It seemed clear as we spoke that he was concerned at how the whole affair was being handled although he did give me the impression that he wasn't particularly surprised.

Reading further documents that were sent by NX after I had asked for them under the Freedom of Information Act, I found a letter stating that the MoD, not me, had asked for this visit. Again, this is not the case. I had taken it upon myself to write directly to DNI as I had previously been in contact with them on several occasions during my previous occupation in HMS *Mercury*.

I wrote to NX on countless occasions asking for someone to travel to my home in order to discuss this case as I was deemed unfit to travel. Norcross had every opportunity to visit me personally from their war pensions branch in Portsmouth which is just nine miles down the road from where I live. NX chose to ignore all such requests, refusing even to acknowledge them as if I had some kind of contagious disease. Despite this being more evidence of the 'wearing down' policy being applied, I remained determined not to let the MoD get the better of me although I was now beginning to wonder how such a high-powered organisation, and I use the word very loosely, could behave in such a bizarre manner and continue to get away with it.

What was concerning me most was my conviction that, had I been an ex-commissioned Royal Navy officer, this state of affairs would never have been allowed to happen. But I persevered. I was one of the three per cent, after all.

I also had three or four telephone conversations with NX, one of which led to my being informed by the young male civil service caller that 'Anyone can make up photographs'. This was after I had provided a photograph of myself sitting on one of *Turpin*'s lower-deck mess decks, alongside another of me standing on the casing (upper deck) with the submarine's name, *TURPIN*, emblazoned above me. At the same time I had also included a copy of the Radio Warfare award board which hung majestically in our Top Secret watch room in HMS *Mercury*. It clearly showed my name, along with that of several others, detailing the awards and commendations that each of us had received after covert operations. But that didn't stop his sarcastic response which hurt. It still does.

At one stage during this marathon, I was given the address of the ICO, the Information Commissioner's Office, to contact to see if they had any qualms about my case and the way the MoD was conducting it. It soon became very apparent that all the ICO were doing was asking questions of the same MoD people I had been in contact with (and getting the same answers) which was enough to give me the distinct impression that this was evidence of yet another bureaucratic and very highly paid quango.

Many of the initial letters I sent to NX were reported as 'not received'. I therefore sent any future correspondence to them by recorded delivery. It seemed, again, to be all part of their 'wearing down' process, another example of which was the way I was treated by some of the doctors NX provided whose understanding of the situation as a whole, as well as their command of the English language, seemed very limited to me. Mind you, one of them did manage to say the word 'fee' very clearly during an otherwise worthless session with him. This sort of treatment made me feel degraded and, ultimately, ashamed to be in the company of someone who was so clearly unable to deal with the matter at hand. NX also continued to refuse, despite evidence to the contrary, to accept that stress can and does lead to heart problems. They claimed my triple heart bypass was probably caused by my smoking, a claim made, no doubt, on the assumption that every member of the Royal Navy smoked.

But I have *never* smoked. In my last ship, of the thirteen senior ratings in my mess, only one occasionally smoked and he, in his own office, on the upper deck. In recent years I have lost my first wife and one of my sisters to smoking. But there seems little wonder that the MoD wouldn't accept that stress was the reason behind my triple heart bypass operation in 1994. If, after all, I was to pass away due to heart-related issues, they would have to pay my dear wife a meagre pension.

At one point, when things were getting rather hot under the collar, NX sent me to see a civilian psychiatrist who was practising in a dilapidated Victorian building in Guildford, a place where NX were obliged to send ex-Royal Navy servicemen. My medical papers would have been held there as well. I should, of course, have been sent to the Royal Naval Hospital Haslar at Gosport which was nearer (26 miles) and more convenient to my home than Guildford (nearly 40 miles). But regulations and no flexibility could be considered here so I was, like everyone else in the position I was now in, sent to Guildford. My wife Margaret, a retired nursing sister, escorted me, as indeed she has to every time I leave our home The psychiatrist who I dealt with said, as she concluded our interview, 'The author of this letter should be sitting where you are, Mr Beasley.'

These senseless games, played out over and over again, were all making my health rapidly deteriorate.

During this time I went to Combat Stress in Leatherhead, a charity that supports servicemen's and servicewomen's mental health. There I heard similar tales from other ex-servicemen, the majority of which were far more traumatic than mine. I eventually became so incensed with what I was hearing that I ceased attending, my departure leading, I hoped, to someone else having the opportunity of spending a couple of weeks or so at this truly idyllic place where one can wander in the woods and enjoy the surrounding countryside with all of its diverse and colourful flora, fauna and, of course and above all, security.

As you will now have realised, my fight for a war pension and some official recognition of what happened to me whilst I was serving on *Turpin* was becoming a very long and drawn-out saga that had now been going on for some years, the full details of which would, believe me, take up many more pages in this book. I have therefore tried to be concise and to give the reader some sort of idea of what I was going through at this time and the obstacles that I was constantly coming up against. Despite all of this I knew that, if I kept on believing that what I was doing was right, there would be a breakthrough. When it eventually came, it was from a most unexpected source.

It was during a particularly bad time that, as I paced my house in the middle of a long and dark night, determined not to take too many painkillers, I hatched a plan. Nothing ventured and nothing gained.

I had, I surmised as I got to work, nothing to lose.

Sitting down, I carefully compiled a three-page dossier noting down much of what you already know. I then sent five prominent people at the time a copy, each of which was accompanied by a different covering letter. The people I chose to write to were as follows:

Margaret Thatcher MP, then the prime minister.
Michael Mates MP, my local member of parliament.
Jack Ashley MP, a committed campaigner for the disabled and their rights
HRH Prince Philip.
One other relevant MP at that time

Five letters, complete with my dossiers, went out. I received five replies. Four of the five concluded that they couldn't (or perhaps wouldn't?) help. But one of the respondents did look take things a little further on my behalf.

My covering letter to HRH had been short and to the point. I'd informed him that, many years previously, I'd been serving onboard HMS *Loch Lomond* in the Mediterranean as a telegraphist. He was, at that time, Lt Prince Philip RN and captain of HMS *Magpie*. His ship had been in need of a temporary telegraphist to replace their own who had been hospitalised. I'd transferred and had spent some time serving on board his ship.

As strategies go, it was a very weak one. But it was sufficient reason for me to write to him. And it worked.

Within a very short time, I received a reply from HRH's press secretary who advised that, whilst HRH himself couldn't assist, he might well know a 'man who can'. Thus, the following day, as I was lounging in the bath in the evening, the telephone rang. Margaret answered and brought the phone to me in the bath, saying, 'A very nice-talking gentleman is asking to speak with you.' After I'd given my name, I was asked a few questions that only I could answer, after which the caller finally asked if I had recently written to anyone connected with royalty.

Once he'd established that I was indeed the person he needed to speak to, he identified himself as Admiral of the Fleet Lord Terence Lewin RN, who had, that morning, received my request by courier via HRH. The admiral went on to say he was concerned with the way I had been treated and added that he would do his best to help, stipulating that he could make no promises. He went on to say that, 'My first port of call will be the archives of the MoD although I fully expect to be refused perusal as these particular patrol and operational reports of HM submarines *Totem* and *Turpin* are probably still classified.'

Within a short time, Lord Lewin rang back to say he had managed to delve into the archives and, a little to his surprise, had 'easily found out' that I *did* serve on submarines during covert operations in the Barents Sea. He would be sending his report to the MoD. The true facts about my service, contained within HMS *Turpin*'s patrol report, were buried deep under the MoD's own feet in the Admiralty archives, the very place where the MoD were conducting this fiasco.

At about the same time, I received a letter from my close mate L/Tel (S) A.D. 'Taffy' Jones who was with me on submarine *Turpin* when my accident in the control room happened. I am at a loss to know how Taff found out about my conflict with the MoD as I'd never told him for the simple reason that I didn't know where he was as we'd not been in touch with each other for a while. Someone up there, it would seem, was looking after me. Taff had always been a good and close friend and had been the best man at my wedding. Needless to say, and as I expected, Taff was very supportive of my case and said he would do all he could to help, although, with the best will in the world, there would have been little he could have practically done. But his friendship meant, as it always had done, a lot to me. Sadly, he and the majority, if not all, of our close-knit team have now passed away. I always remember during his best man speech at our wedding he had said, in a hesitant Welsh accent that, 'If it hadn't been for Tony, we both wouldn't be here today.' I still most certainly am and owe that fact to my dear wife and my daughter, who is a doctor.

***

I ultimately succeeded with, as a representative of the Royal British Legion described it, my 'impossible aim'. Yet this had come at a terrible cost to both my state of health and my financial standing. My health has suffered greatly throughout this totally unnecessary saga, my resolve gradually worn down in all of my dealings with people who I can only describe as the public puppets of the hidden mandarins who are tucked away, along with all the archives, deep within the MoD. History now dictates that no one will ever admit to the charade which followed my attempt to establish a little justice and fair play because, way back at the beginning, it would have taken just one visit from Norcross NX to my home for them to establish the truth. They would then have been in receipt of the correct facts in hand, and would have been able to spare me the stress and trauma which eventually led to a triple heart bypass, during which, as I lay on the operating table, I almost lost my life.

I never had the courtesy of such a visit. But I should add at this point that an ex-commissioned officer would most certainly have received one at their home.

Soon after NX were, eventually, forced to pay me a war pension, I was handed a shabby piece of A4 paper which gave me priority treatment in hospital for any treatment I may require which is attributable to the injuries for which the war pension was paid. It stated:

> PTSD – Post Traumatic Stress Disorder, including panic attacks. Cervical Spondylosis, Osteoarthritis, back and shoulders.

I have, on two occasions, attempted to use this MoD 'priority' and, on two occasions, have been looked at as if I was something that the anchor had dragged up. Things got no better for all this, though. I cannot always use my right hand very well for simple things like answering the telephone or cutting meat at mealtimes. I used to read the *Daily Telegraph*; however, I now find it difficult to hold, due to its size. Fortunately, the *i* newspaper and *Channel Four* provide me with all the news I want to hear and, as for my hands and fingers, I continue to find that touch typing is a good therapy.

I have no qualms about the eventual war pension I was awarded. My complaint was the way it had to be achieved in the first place.

Epilogue

The Cold War feels like a period from ancient history now, but anyone who lived through those times will remember the very real fear that the world was going to end in nuclear confrontation between East and West. The Soviet Union was a strong and implacable enemy, and the war against it was fought on many fronts, largely under conditions of the utmost secrecy. My posting aboard HMS *Turpin* played an important part in that war: GCHQ and the MoD were so desperate to acquire one specific radio intercept that they were prepared to sacrifice our lives and vessel in order to get it. I did the work I was on board HMS *Turpin* to do and was fortunate enough to know, then and now, that it was a job of work that was extremely well done.

The injury to my neck had occurred as I was falling to the deck after my tussle with a ton and a half of periscope after *Turpin* made its crash dive, avoiding, in the process, an instant ramming and destruction from a Russian destroyer. We were lucky, very lucky. Often, whenever my pain becomes almost a little too intense to bear, the memory of this incident immediately flashes up in my mind. It is now, and will always be, intertwined with all the mental agony I have been forced to endure ever since by a system that is clearly unfit for purpose.

I left the Royal Navy as a master-at-arms. It is an equivalent rank to, for example, a regimental sergeant major in the British Army. It is, rank-wise, as high as you can possibly go in the service without breaking through the glass ceiling and entering the rarefied world of the commissioned officer. It is, for any non-commissioned man or woman, a very considerable achievement which results in your being given a position of no little responsibility.

But you are still not an officer and must, therefore, do without all the rights and privileges afforded to them. You are, in other words, and remain, an 'ordinary' soldier rather than a 'gentleman'.

This predicament was something which was recognised by one of the great men of the senior service, Lord Louis Mountbatten. I had, in 1974, the very great pleasure of being in his company, together with several other chief petty officers. We were all, as usual and with Mountbatten fully engaged in the conversation, putting the services to rights when, quite unexpectedly, Lord Louis said, 'If all of you had been in the British Army, you would have had a commission long ago.'

With what the great man said always at the back of my mind, I made sure that, throughout my long battle against the forces of Norcross NX, I frequently asked why we 'other ranks' were always treated differently to the commissioned officers. On each and every occasion, my question was ignored. There is, without any doubt, a difference, and this has now been the case for far too long. I can cite one example here, and now, the awards given for injury are always higher for an officer than they are for an ordinary serving soldier. As we head towards the third decade of the twenty-first century, we are still living and working with the same doctrine in these matters that was applied in the First World War. It beggars belief.

I am currently in receipt of an 80 per cent war pension. And this may appear, on the outside, to be satisfactory. My ongoing concern is the way that award was, ultimately, achieved, and the consequent and continuing health problems I sustained in eventually getting it.

Acknowledgements

I would like to thank my wife Margaret for all of the love and support she has always given me.

Tony Beasley

Tony has given me the opportunity to share and help retell his remarkable story, I will forever be indebted to him for doing so.

The generosity of spirit he and Margaret have shown me, their excellent company, support and co-operation during the whole of this project will be something I never forget. I very much hope to continue to enjoy their company and conversation for many years to come.

My thanks to Daniel Tidbury of Tidbury Media for his support and valued input and expertise.

Sincere thanks also to Isobel Fulton, Felicity Goldsack and Ruth Sheppard of Casemate Publishers for their support and backing which is hugely appreciated.

Edward Couzens-Lake